THE METHOD TO THE MAGIC

GROWING RAINMAKERS

A GUIDE TO BUILDING A GREAT SALES TEAM THAT THRIVES IN THE MODERN MARKETPLACE

DAVE WILENS

INDIE BOOKS
INTERNATIONAL

ISBN-10: 1-947480-50-2
ISBN-13: 978-1-947480-50-6
Library of Congress Control Number: 2019934188

Designed by Joni McPherson, mcphersongraphics.com
Author cover photo by Amanda Wilens

INDIE BOOKS INTERNATIONAL, LLC
2424 VISTA WAY, SUITE 316
OCEANSIDE, CA 92054
www.indiebooksintl.com

Rainmakers

Definition: People who generate significant income for a business or organization by attracting clients or customers.

PRAISE FOR
GROWING RAINMAKERS

"*Coach's methodology helps you engage with emotional honesty and enthusiasm to any client or prospect and this makes your life relationships and business richer for it. Having applied his guidance in the past in a continental sales leadership role, I know it works personally. Seeing his influence on my new company's sales people demonstrated that you can invest to sharpen presentation skills to grow rainmakers.*"

MICHAEL A. CHUBB, GENERAL MANAGER,
THE SASKATOON COLOSTRUM COMPANY

"*To build a great sales team you first need to be a great sales manager/coach. This book shows us what a sales manager needs to do in an engaging story format. Great read for anyone in the C-suite who wants to understand how to build an outstanding sales team. It starts with one person, the sales manager. Give him/her this book!*"

JEFFREY GRUBBS, COO/CFO, BICKMORE RISK SERVICES

"*A quick, easy and thought-provoking read that provides a concise and usable roadmap to turning sales people into successful rainmakers. On a personal note, while I was reading it I gained a much better appreciation for why the CEO shouldn't be the sales manager.*"

ALLAN HENRIQUES, CHAIRMAN OF THE BOARD,
SMART INVESTOR

"Your efforts to pay it forward by sharing your insights are indeed admirable. There's an awful lot of well-established truth in the words that you've committed to paper. I simply hope that, with the accelerating shifts in our culture (and away from how business used to be done), there are enough people to take the time to read, digest and ultimately benefit from the truths that you've been willing to share."

PAUL LELIAKOV, PAST PRESIDENT, THE MONEY STORE
COMMERCIAL LENDING DIVISION

CONTENTS

FOREWORD

When I first dipped my toe into the world of sales, I admittedly had no idea what a *rainmaker* was. Aside from the obvious Native American origins of the word, which describe a member of a tribe who dances in the fields to magically summon the clouds to bring rain for the crops, all I could glean from the context is that a rainmaker was a really good salesperson who was naturally gifted at closing sales.

Growing up in a family where I could "do anything I put my mind to," the idea of being this sort of rainmaker didn't sit well with me. I realized at a young age that if I wanted to be a great trumpet player, I only needed to practice long, hard, and smart enough, and I would inevitably reach my goal. I was not a naturally-gifted musical prodigy, and therefore had to follow an organized and structured practice regimen on a daily basis to get where I wanted to go. I was not a naturally-gifted rainmaker in the business world, either, but I was determined to get as close as possible.

When I first started business development coaching sessions in his Coffee with Coach program, Dave Wilens set the record straight: a rainmaker is a good salesperson, but a good salesperson is not necessarily a rainmaker. To that end, a good salesperson simply makes sales, but a rainmaker establishes a deep, meaningful relationship with their clients and prospects, allowing them to access revenue streams and make sales as if by magic. But, the good news is this: there is a method to the magic, and that method is carefully and thoughtfully laid out in the following pages.

I encourage you to take the *Growing Rainmakers* method to heart and apply Dave's step-by-step tactics to every aspect of your business. What makes this book useful is that the strategies and takeaways are timeless and actionable and can be incorporated into your everyday routine. Whether you are of the millennial, Gen X/Y, or boomer generation, and whether you are a salesperson, sales manager, business owner, executive or the like, you will find that Dave lays the concepts out in a relatable story featuring all sorts of characters we all come across in our everyday business life. If you're like me, this book will prove to be your invaluable guide to becoming a rainmaker by developing vital, lasting relationships with your clients.

Rachel Freeman of Smart Investor
September 2018
Roseville, California

PREFACE

Everyone knows that no one gets paid until a sale is made. If sales aren't being made, the company will inevitably fold.

Just as human bodies rely on the heart to keep blood circulating throughout the body, companies rely on sales to keep revenue circulating throughout the business.

A friend and mentor of mine, Jack Daly, says:

"There are three sins a company makes with the position of sales management:

1. The CEO is the sales manager.

2. Leadership promotes the best salesperson (the rainmaker) to be the sales manager.

3. They require the new rainmaker sales manager to also carry a book of business."

I have seen all three of these scenarios multiple times in a variety of industries and it has caused many failures.

In the years I have been working with companies of all different sizes, I have uncovered another common thread: sales managers are rarely trained or prepared to do their job. To this day, I continue to be surprised and perplexed by this reality. Since sales are a vital element of any successful business, how could such an important position like sales management be left to chance? I have noted that many business owners don't consider the position of sales manager as a key position, and this is a major error.

Beyond the basic concepts of supply and demand, a business owner must understand related concepts, specifically marginal revenue. A thorough grasp of marginal revenue can help decision-makers within the business make informed decisions concerning changes in production. The potential benefits and consequences of this economic concept also need to be part of each rainmaker's knowledge base in regard to pricing. Always keep in mind that if profitable revenue is not increasing, the business will struggle and eventually fail.

In the United States, many universities offer degrees in Sales and Marketing. Looking carefully at these curriculums, they focus heavily on the marketing aspect of revenue generation. I am excited to see that a few universities have recently begun to offer a variety of certificates in sales and marketing at various levels. The H.H. Gregg Center at Ball State University in Muncie, Indiana continues to be recognized as one of the nation's best sales centers and is among an elite handful accredited by the University Sales Center Alliance* They offer a new program that provides the opportunity for students to excel with a bachelor's degree in Professional Selling. Besides traditional professors, Ball State provides the students a chance to work with sales coaches from the industry. It's awesome to see that schools of higher education are catching up with the times.

While we are on the right path to educate and train our young people to become professionals in the field of sales and sales management, there is a huge void in the marketplace. Sales forces need to be educated and trained now. We need rainmakers on our sales forces because every business is being put to the test of pricing challenges presented by the internet, increased competition from innovative companies, international competition, new technologies, the aging populations of our workforce, hiring the next generation, and our internal staffs that don't want to change the way things have always been done. So, beyond formal education and training, there is a need for the experienced, successful relationship-sales-superstars to share their secret sauce, and not only allow but encourage the young, new talent to bring their flare to the process. Together, this key aspect of talent development can and will improve it. In other words, you really can't grow rainmakers unless you are willing to bridge the generational gap.

Dan Larson is a colleague and friend of mine that refers to connecting the dots between marketing and sales. He explains that a healthy business is like a race car with all four wheels needing to move at the same pace. One wheel is Marketing, one is Leads, another is Sales, and the fourth wheel is Operations. All four wheels are fueled by Finance and driven by Systems and Processes. If any one of those wheels starts to rotate at a different speed, the race car sputters, performs poorly, or worse, goes out of control and crashes. If there is a breakdown in the power source or control systems, the race car slows down, swerves out of control, or stops.

How marketing generates the leads, how operations fulfills the sales orders, the attitude of our internal staff, logistics, how to project profitability, and what cash flow is necessary to support sales are for other books.

In this book, you are going to meet a variety of characters I have experienced while on the road as a sales coach.

My hope is the stories I will share in this book will remind you of people you know, possibly work with, and perhaps have done business with in some form or another. My reflections are provided to help you gain an understanding of the necessary attitude, skills, and activities that are needed to grow rainmakers. I will cover the five focus areas for sales managers to building a championship team, including:

1. Hiring the Best People

2. Starting them Successfully

3. Training and Educating

4. Continual Growth and Developing

5. Keeping the Best People

As Jim Collins said in his #1 Bestseller, *From Good to Great*, "You must have the right people on the bus and have them in the right seat."

Dave Wilens
September 2018
Sacramento, California

Joe —
I am honored to be introduced to you. What a wonderful bio, I'm look foreword to hearing the stories behind the timeline. Enjoy the read, you are a Rainmaker!

Best
coach
Paul
5/2019

---

* In April 2002, representatives from nine universities met during the National Conference on Sales Management to develop an organization that would increase the professionalism of the sales field, improve the status of sales as an academic discipline, and assist other universities in this mission. Playing a key role in the development of what would become the University Sales Center Alliance were representatives of Ball State University, Baylor University, Illinois State University, Kennesaw State University, Northern Illinois University, Ohio University, University of Akron, University of Houston and University of Toledo.

THE STORY BEGINS

1 | Meet Olivia, Our Hero

One résumé that stood out from the pile on the sales manager's desk was from a young woman named Olivia, who had recently graduated college and had tons of sales experience for someone her age.

Jeremy, the sales manager, immediately sent her an email requesting an interview.

One thing that Jeremy knew for sure was that he really wanted to fill in some of the void on his sales team with young blood. This would give the team someone that he could mold, a young person with energy, a direct report who understood new technologies, social media, and a person who wanted a career and would stick around for the long haul.

Across town, when Olivia received Jeremy's email, inviting her to interview for a B2B sales job at a food distribution company that specialized selling to restaurants, she was ecstatic.

Later that week, when Olivia walked into Jeremy's office, he knew from the moment he saw her that she would be perfect. There was a level of self-confidence that he had not seen in many people her age.

As they talked, it became obvious to Jeremy that Olivia was the life of the party. "As a young child," Olivia said, "people were always telling me I was a natural saleswoman. I was never at a lack of something to say; I had the gift of gab." Within a few hours, the two seemed like old friends. Jeremy sold Olivia on how great the company was to work for, the career path she would be on, and the potential earnings she could achieve.

As for experience, Olivia's first job had been the summer after high school. A national department store hired her to sell clothing, and she did a great job. Olivia spent the next five years attending a local state university earning her BA in Communications, minoring in business. She worked several part-time, sales-oriented jobs to help support herself while in school.

The hiring process she went through took a couple of hours of chatting together in Jeremy's office, followed by a brief tour of the sales department. They then went out to lunch where Jeremy filled her head with his personal experiences in sales, highlighting his personal achievements and sharing the story of his professional rise to the top in the few short years he had been at QAZ foods.

Jeremy asked Olivia if she had a big dream.

"My dream is to become a great rainmaker, and to reward myself with my dream car, a 1969 Chevy Camaro."

"If you think a '69 Chevy Camaro is great," said Jeremy, "let me tell you about my Porsche."

He prattled on and on about his car, and then got back to sales.

"I think what you are saying is you want to be a great salesman, like me," said Jeremy.

"A great saleswoman has a nice ring to it," said Olivia.

"I promise that if you take this, you will get a great territory with plenty of solid customers, and I will personally see to your training," said Jeremy.

They reviewed the current compensation package again.

"I'd like you to know that I am going to change the commission in the near future," said Jeremy. "This new plan is going to give you more upside potential."

At the end of lunch, Olivia was officially offered the position and enthusiastically accepted.

"When do I start?" said Olivia, thrusting out her hand to shake on the deal.

"Report to the HR office next Monday morning."

RAINMAKER PRINCIPLES
CHAPTER 1

- Ideal personality characteristics for a potential rainmaker are to be self-confident, energetic, and outgoing.

- People do things for their own reasons, not yours, so choosing candidates with big goals is a must for sales recruitments with rainmaker potential.

2 | Jeremy, The "Rock Star"

J eremy walked with a swagger that showed he was full of self-confidence—to the point of being a bit cocky. He was smooth in every aspect, from his manner of dress to his obvious flirtatious chivalry, to his quick answers to any questions asked on any subject. The big beautiful house in a high-end suburb of Chicago, a Lexus convertible, great wardrobe, and membership at a private country club paint the remaining picture of Jeremy.

Back in the days when he was attending university, Jeremy worked part-time in the kitchen of the union cafeteria. It was enjoyable work for him because he loved food. Starting as an assistant, he worked his way through most of the back-of-the-house positions and by his senior year became the purchasing manager. Working with suppliers to keep the pantry well stocked and the costs down was a pretty cool job for him. He was learning the tricks of the trade that would be of benefit to any restaurant. The satisfaction of successfully doing his job was only outdone by the feeling of success and power achieved from the authority he had to make decisions on his own.

Upon achieving his undergraduate degree in communications, Jeremy began his working career doing what he knew in a restaurant kitchen. He wore many hats for this medium size business, eventually becoming the supply chain manager. It was here that he realized that the people who were making the big money were either the owners or those who sold the food to the owners.

The next career move was simple: he needed to become a salesman. At first, he struggled to land a job selling in the food industry because he lacked the necessary sales skills, experience, and connections. Needing to earn a living, Jeremy accepted an offer and hit the road, learning the sales game through the world of the wholesale hardware industry. Selling everything from nuts to bolts was his realm for the next year. Covering a rather large territory in the Midwest was good for a start, and he met a lot of great people along the way. Kevin, the eldest son of a restaurant owner, was one of them, who, interestingly enough, was working as a sales representative for a food distribution company.

Through Kevin's introduction, Jeremy landed a sales position with one of the largest food distributors in the country. Understanding the inner workings of restaurant and commercial kitchens combined with his exaggerated sales experience gave him an advantage that most of the other new hires didn't possess.

The sixty-day training period filled his head with product knowledge, learning about the systems and processes to service customers, and guided him how to get through the various hurdles of working in a large corporation. The most boring part of his training was either learning about all the varieties of french fries and string beans that they offered or the introduction to the CRM (Customer Relationship Management) software program. To Jeremy, this was basically the system used by the company to keep an eye on his activities. You know, Big-Brother-Is-Watching type of software. But, while talking to staff that was already out there selling, he learned that most of them don't use it, anyway.

On the first day of his third month, he found himself riding with one of the seasoned sales pros to gain an understanding of the day-to-day operations he would be performing. Over the next few weeks, he rode with numerous people who were in his assigned district. They each did things a little differently, worked at various levels of intensity, and were all very proud of their achievements, no matter how large or small. They spent time checking customers' inventory, trying to get chefs to buy products that they currently purchased from the competition, and cold calling. Eventually Jeremy spent a couple of days in the field with the sales manager. He passed this test with flying colors and was assigned a number of accounts and a physical territory that he was responsible for developing.

With his outgoing personality, confidence, and the understanding of how successful restaurants are run, he was very effective right out of the gate. Earning large commission checks, winning bonuses for various contests, and gaining admission to the president's club every year became an expected achievement. After rising to the top of sales on a national level in just five short years, he earned a promotion to sales manager—a change in position that offered great opportunities for wealth and happiness, yet it destroyed a friendship he'd had since his days as a road-warrior selling hardware.

The raise in base pay over his old salary was minimal compared to the new status he had accomplished. After all, he was still able to earn top commission and compete in contests for the sales he made. Plus, he received a piece of the action from the rest of his team. Life was good for Jeremy the Rock Star, and everybody knew it.

As sales manager, his workload didn't change much. He kept most of his customers because they had been with him from the start. In retrospect, they were mostly the founders' customers that were handed down to his predecessors and eventually turned over to him. Now this is not to say that he wasn't responsible for bringing on new business or that he wasn't able to build more sales from the existing customers. He generated sales from everywhere. Jeremy even held a company record of saving 90 percent of the customers when other salespeople moved on to new opportunities or switched to a competitor. He was a great relationship builder; his stories had a sense of humor to them and people like to associate with a winner.

The job instructions he received from the Vice President of Sales and Marketing on his first day as sales manager were short and sweet. "Do what you have always done and show other people how to do it." It was almost that simple, with a short list of management tasks and responsibilities. He now had to decide who would take the new customers that had called in looking to open an account, share the monthly sales numbers with the team while holding their feet to the fire, make decisions on pricing, conduct sales meetings, hire new salespeople, and of course, fire those who didn't hit their goals.

Not only was life good for Jeremy, but it was getting better. As the sales manager, he was able to take more customers out golfing, to lunch, or to nice dinners. Not just his own, but the top customers for other salespeople and their top prospects, too. While he was entertaining, he had the power to give special pricing and terms, therefore landing even more sales than ever. His sense of self-worth was exploding, and at the same time that his sales were climbing, he expected better results from his previous teammates. The once self-confident sales leader, the guy everyone else wanted to emulate, had changed, and no one on the team liked it.

RAINMAKER PRINCIPLES
CHAPTER 2

- A great way to bring on the right person is through personal referrals. It is much more effective than help-wanted ads or online recruiting services.

- Many companies use old-fashioned training methods from yesteryear. The best companies incorporate e-learning, other multimedia formats, and outsourced coaching from experts. Combining these alternatives with the existing in-house training methods improves results and provides measurable accountability metrics.

- Traditionally, it has been the job of the sales manager to grow sales, no matter what they decide to do, how they do it, or who makes the sale. In the modern marketplace, the focus of the sales manager is to grow their sales people.

- The same modern management philosophy to grow your people is transferable across all departments. High-performing companies are those that invest in their people.

PART II

THE CRISIS

3 | Trying to Clone Rock Stars

Why were all the salespeople leaving?

Within a few months of Jeremy's promotion, his old friend Kevin resigned and left town without so much as a goodbye. He was the one who had introduced Jeremy to the company, and his peer that helped him get his start at QAZ. They hung out socially and worked well together right up until the promotion. Honestly, Jeremy couldn't bring himself to care much. "If Kevin wasn't willing to get in line, straighten up, fly right, and respect the new boss, then he must not have been a friend worth having in the first place."

Then within a few weeks, another veteran salesman resigned as well, a guy the CEO called his rainmaker. He had been with the company for twelve years, in the industry for his entire career, had a good book of business, and had built many strong relationships with customers over the years. Knowing for a while that he couldn't take it much longer, he found a position with one of the company's competitors and successfully moved half of his customers with him.

While this was a serious blow to sales, Jeremy didn't accept any of the responsibility. He told his boss and the sales team, "That guy was an old dog. He didn't move fast enough, didn't keep up with technology and he stopped hunting for new business. We can replace him easily." Jeremy was confident that he would make up for the loss before the end of the year, and get all the customers back from the competition.

Two weeks later, two other employees gave Jeremy formal letters of resignation.

Still, Jeremy didn't think much of the development, even though the now ex-salespeople had complained to everyone who would listen (including during sales meetings) about how difficult it was becoming to make sales recently. Most sales staff agreed. They were all concerned because they weren't making enough money even though they were all sharing territories that were larger due to the recent departures.

During exit interviews with the HR department, Kevin and the others who had resigned recently had been quite frank.

"Working for Jeremy isn't easy. He expects a lot and he takes all of the good customers for himself."

"No matter who we talk to about the difficult conditions for salespeople here, it's quite apparent that nothing is ever going to change."

"Jeremy doesn't support us. He competes with us. It's impossible to succeed when your boss is your number one competitor."

All the dissatisfaction shared by the sales team was just considered "water cooler talk," and the other managers and the boss simply ignored it all.

With the salesforce quickly dwindling, Jeremy had no choice but to hire some fresh blood. He immediately began writing help-wanted ads. His plan was to put the ads in free or inexpensive options such as Craigslist, listings at the local college or other free online job posting sites, for starters. If that didn't get him the right results, then he would expand the search to high profile pay sites like Monster, LinkedIn, Indeed and CareerBuilder, to name a few. As with most things in life, it was easy for him to describe the great opportunity he had for a Business Development Position:

> Our company has been in business since 1959. We have a great product line, one of the strongest online reputations and the highest quality customer service scores in the industry. When you join our team, your mission will be to help us become the number one operating company in the region. This is a great position that offers extremely competitive wages, health benefits, 401K on top of performance bonuses with an uncapped earning potential. What we're looking for:
>
> • **Restaurant or commercial kitchen experience**
>
> • **Strong interpersonal skills**
>
> • **Customer service focus**
>
> • **Strong work ethic, self-motivated and goal-oriented**

- Excellent writing and oral communication skills

- Candidate must be reliable and punctual

- Competitive and positive attitude

- Ability to learn quickly

- Understand successful sales techniques

- Technologically savvy

- Work in a positive team environment, monthly bonuses, prizes, great career growth potential, management opportunities and extensive training.

Almost immediately, the phone began to ring off the hook with people looking for a job and wanting to apply.

Not being able to deal with the swarm of people who wanted to work for him, Jeremy quickly changed the advertisement, removing the phone number and directing prospective new hires to submit their résumés via email. Once this was under control, he was able to get back to his regular work—seeing his customers, along with any of the good customers that had belonged to the four salespeople who had resigned.

By the next day, Jeremy was confident this was a great move and a fantastic opportunity for the company. He would find a couple of energetic new people—people who didn't have bad habits—he could easily train to be just like him. Sales would begin to soar once again.

RAINMAKER PRINCIPLES
CHAPTER 3

- Promoting a top salesperson to sales manager is a mistake, especially when:

  - The company asks them to carry their own book of business.

  - The company pays them to double dip on commissions, both their own sales and the people they manage.

  - The company doesn't provide guidelines, set expectations or measure results other than the department's financial goals.

  - The company doesn't provide sales specific management training or any management training that has a focus on individual and team growth.

4 | Meet Earl, The *Other* Sales Guy

E arl really wasn't prepared to look for a new job, but he wasted little time putting together a résumé and combing the help-wanted ads.

With a wife, two adult children and ten years left until retirement, Earl was under great pressure when his employer decided to close the doors. He began this job fifteen years ago as a beverage and restaurant delivery driver. Besides delivering products, he had the additional responsibility to check the customers' inventory and order necessary replacements. He was a great guy that loved to golf and fish, got along with almost everyone, and after a few years had built enough customer relationships that he was promoted into sales. This job was easy for him because he was essentially doing the same work as before—except now he got to drive a company car, walk in the front door, shoot the breeze with his buddies and eat breakfast, lunch, or an occasional dinner at the customer's establishment. Life was good for years...until the doors closed.

Earl even called and visited a few of his old customers to see if they knew of any opportunities. After a few months, his attitude was beginning to shift so he took a break to hit the links. Wouldn't you know that by the fifth hole his wife called with the news that she had seen the perfect job listing for him on Craigslist? It was in the same industry, offered great pay, full benefits, and more.

He told her immediately to send them his résumé, and he would try to find out who they were when he was finished with his round.

As luck would have it, he received an email reply from the sales manager that evening. The sales manager indicated a strong interest in meeting him in person and included instructions for Earl to take some kind of online assessment. So, Earl immediately logged in. Twenty minutes later, he was done. He must have given the right answers. The following morning, he received another email asking him to call the main phone number of QAZ Food Distributors to schedule an interview with HR and the sales manager.

The interview with a human resources representative went well, but when he met with Jeremy, it was off-the-charts successful. They had tons of connections in common. Both were golfers. And although Jeremy didn't ever go fishing, he said he was interested in going out to catch the big one someday. Jeremy told Earl how great QAZ Food Distributors were, and why they had always been such tough competitors of his before. He already knew a great deal of their product lines. While he realized that he may not get all his old customers assigned to him, he was sure to get some of them. The base pay and commissions were different than at his previous job, and Jeremy mentioned that he was working on a new structure that would give Earl even more upside potential. At the end of the interview, they shook hands on the deal. Earl felt that they had known each other for years. The newest QAZ Food Distributor's employee would start the very next Monday.

While Earl was celebrating his new position, Jeremy continued to read résumés and interview other candidates. After all, he had lost three solid sales performers. As much as Jeremy believed he made a great hire, he knew that even someone with Earl's experience wasn't going to fill the gap completely.

In his mind, Earl was an old dog expecting to service his old customers, and not hunt for new business. Jeremy's plan didn't exactly line up with that thinking. Sure, he was going to give him a few of the old customers, but primarily the small accounts that didn't have great potential.

Let's face it, Jeremy thought, Earl was going to be challenged in many ways to keep up with this Rock Star manager who knew everything.

RAINMAKER PRINCIPLES
CHAPTER 4

- Don't hire a person to simply fill an empty seat or because you have a few outside interests in common.

- Don't hire a person because of their experience alone, what they put on their résumé or because of their personal image.

- Personality and Emotional Intelligence Assessments are useful tools to help identify if a prospective employee fits the culture of the company and the position they will be assigned to. However, using the results of these two tests alone should not be used to make a manager's hiring decision. The results should carry a weight of approximately 30 percent into a manager's decision-making process.

- You should only hire someone that you believe would bring value to the team or someone that is going to improve the performance gaps.

- If you are planning on changing the compensation plan, do it prior to offering the position to someone. Once it's set, don't change it! Sales people usually feel management is punishing them for their previous successes, though the company feels the sales people are getting paid too much for meeting or exceeding the company's targets. It is a mistake to change compensation due to successful sales results.

5 | Basic Training for Olivia and Earl

O livia and Earl spent most of their first day filling out HR forms and getting introduced to the office staff at QAZ Foods.

The operation was big, and according to Earl, nothing was similar to his old company. Obviously, it was all new to Olivia. The phones were ringing constantly in the order department where some fifty employees were frantically taking and placing orders. The operation was buzzing with activity, and every aspect of the inside order department appeared to run with efficiency. They definitely knew how to stay productive and were held to very high-performance standards that the corporation instilled in them.

On day two, Earl and Olivia joined a half a dozen other new recruits and were given a tour of the dry, wet, refrigeration, and freezer warehouses. Once again, this proved to be an overwhelming experience, and everyone felt the excitement of being a part of this team. There was a brief meeting with Jeremy on Wednesday morning. Then they were split up as Earl was teamed up with Laura, another team member who would show him the ropes at QAZ. Meanwhile, Olivia and the others were placed in a product training room with Ralph, a gentleman who was rather slow-moving but seemed very knowledgeable about the merchandise QAZ Foods sold.

It was amazing, and at the same time daunting, to learn about how many varieties of common products they carried. For example, there are thirty-two varieties of french fries, forty-eight cuts of green beans, and an endless choice of many other foods.

After the first two weeks, Olivia was almost completely checked out mentally. However, the company's product-training program was scheduled to last a full eight weeks. There was still a great deal to learn. She told herself to focus and felt the need to just keep pushing forward. Internally, while she was already doubting her career choice, she was able to reaffirm her commitment to the program the very next weekend. She reflected to understand that the 250-plus salespeople and the eighteen sales managers currently out in the field had gone through the exact same training before her. If they could do it, so could she. After all, she was a natural and would someday become rich with commissions and bonuses. She would learn these products, pass the exams, and be assigned a great territory upon graduation. She set her sights on becoming the first person to earn the President's Achievement Award for sales during her rookie year.

Occasionally during her training, Olivia ran into Earl. From time to time, he was in-house doing desk work or picking up product for a customer. He seemed to be doing okay and was impressed with the field training he was receiving from Laura. She was always upbeat and had great relationships with her customers.

After a few weeks Earl said he felt he was ready to go out and start working in his own territory. Heck, he thought, he missed some of his old buddies who had been his customers from his previous company. On top of the social aspect of reconnecting, he also really needed to get out to earn some commissions. Unfortunately, as a seasoned salesman, he wasn't even offered the same base pay as a new trainee. The majority of his pay was based on his sales. He quoted Jeremy's words upon hiring him: "You eat what you kill! That's the only way a good salesman wants to work—on commission!"

Curiously, Olivia didn't see Jeremy for days at a time. It appeared that he spent most of his time out of the building, working as a producer. She remembered him telling her during the interview process that being number one on the sales team was still his personal driver. He obviously worked hard to achieve this honor, and nothing was going to get in his way. Maybe his base pay as manager was bigger than Earl's, but obviously he wanted to eat what he killed, too.

The start of Olivia's new career was nothing like she had imagined it would be. After all, in her interview she had been told she would be able to interact with the customers and begin making sales from the start. She became even more disengaged when she remembered being told how she was going to be introduced to the customers she would be working with in her new territory.

Olivia was more than eager to get out and make some meaningful contributions.

Just about the time she was ready to explode from restlessness, Olivia was invited to her first sales meeting. She was introduced to the team as the newest sales associate. Receiving a round of applause for graduating from the eight-week training class in just five weeks, the congratulations from the team made her feel welcome and energized. Finally, she was going to be given the chance to actually interact with others, sell something, and actually earn some commissions.

The Friday afternoon meeting began with Jeremy going over the sales numbers from the previous month. A few of the individual salespeople were up, but no one was as high above target as the bossman. The feeling that he was almost taunting the other sales associates felt strange to Olivia. When he got down to the people at the bottom of the performance list, things got more intense. Jeremy was practically belittling them for not working hard enough, and not making enough cold calls. He was unquestionably ridiculing their sales abilities. Making these associates feel inferior was a much different approach to leading or helping people become successful than she had ever experienced. Through her involvement in sports, music, other jobs, working with her father as a kid on their car rebuilding projects, and all of her schooling, Olivia had never experienced this type of mentorship or management. Of course, she wasn't worried about herself in the future. Clearly, she thought, she would never be in an unproductive position. That said, Olivia still felt bad for the people on the receiving end of Jeremy's sarcasm and belittling.

The last hour of the meeting focused primarily on some new programs being introduced by a couple of the food manufacturers and brokers. Then there were some pricing changes on some of the existing product lines and various other updates. Finally, Jeremy gave Earl his own territory and customer list. Then he assigned Olivia to start her outside sales training with one of the other associates—one who was always up near the top of the charts. She couldn't have wished for a better person to shadow.

Overall, Olivia felt it had been a rather dull and demoralizing meeting. Of course, with her positive, can-do attitude, the newest sales associate was able to put it all behind her and walk out looking forward to a great weekend ahead. Time to reinvigorate, generate positive vibes, review some of the product changes that had just been given out to the team, and prepare for Monday morning.

RAINMAKER PRINCIPLES
CHAPTER 5

- Most people in their first thirty days of employment are concerned that they made a mistake by taking the new job. There are a number of onboarding guidelines that should be followed:
  - A manager should never start new hires unless he/she is available to spend time for orientation and to make them feel welcome.
  - Product training is an essential element for most jobs, but don't burn out your new hires. Mix product training with other subjects.
  - Provide an existing staff member as a buddy to help the new hire adapt easier.
  - A manager should check in daily with the new hire to keep a pulse on progress and attitude.
- Sales meetings or any departmental meetings are not conducted to ridicule and belittle weak performers. This should never be done, especially publicly. The purpose of departmental meetings should focus on staff growth, development, encouraging positive results, and for teaching and communicating important information.

6 | Into the Field Training

Jake, the associate assigned to field train Olivia, contacted her over the weekend with orders to meet him at 7:00 a.m. sharp at the Starbucks on Milwaukee Avenue. She was eager to finally embark on her new career and was up with the sun that morning. She dressed in a fashionable, but practical, black pantsuit that would be warm in cold refrigerated areas and rubber-soled, non-slip flats that would be secure on potentially wet surfaces.

This was it. The day she would go out into the real world of sales. She couldn't wait to meet up with Jake.

Olivia arrived fifteen minutes early and he was already there, gulping from a Venti something-or-other and busily working on his laptop. "Olivia! Good morning. You'll be riding along for the next few days. Jeremy wanted me to show you the ropes because I became a top producer after just four years in this company and industry. On Friday, I'm going to give him a debrief, and depending on what I say, you'll either ride along with one of the other guys next, or Jeremy himself may decide to take you out. Go ahead and get yourself something to wake you up. We have some planning to do."

The next two hours consisted of Olivia looking over Jake's shoulder at various notebooks and the CRM as he developed his plan of attack for the day. She asked a few questions, but mostly, she tried to make intuitive sense of his approach through shadowing and observation.

Jake's first order of business was to drive out to a long-time account of his that had started buying more products from one of the local produce companies. The plan was to sit down to have a nice breakfast and then talk with his good friend, the chef. If everything went as planned, the customer would be introduced to and convinced to try their new Value Add Produce Program. This program featured many organic products, two deliveries per week, and had special pricing.

That was the plan, at least. While they enjoyed a great breakfast at the restaurant, unfortunately the chef was too busy to talk because his line cook and one other person from the kitchen staff hadn't shown up for work that day. Full of hearty omelets and toast, they waved goodbye and headed out to their next stop, the largest senior care facility in the area.

The drive to the facility was about forty-five minutes, and they listened to sports radio the entire way there. It turned out that her new mentor was really into sports, especially the Cubs and Bulls. Other than stock car races, which she had attended faithfully with her dad while growing up, Olivia couldn't care less about spectator sports. So, she checked news, social media, and work email on her cell phone while Jake focused intently on the previous day's games, scores, stats, analysis, and speculation about who might make it to the playoffs this year.

Upon arrival at the senior care facility, Olivia was wowed at the size and scope of the kitchen. Going right to work, they did a walk-though inventory, discussed the results with the manager, and placed a nice order for delivery the following morning. With this sale under their belt, it was time to drop by a new sandwich shop that was about to open in the same area.

Regrettably, the owner wasn't at the shop when they arrived. There were only a few construction people and a city inspector onsite. While Jake hadn't met the owner yet, he told Olivia he stopped by a couple times a week with the hope that he would catch the owner one of these days. "Cold calling isn't my favorite thing to do," said Jake, "but since Jeremy requires it, I do just enough of it to cover my tail."

The rest of the morning was spent filling out details for the big order and making several phone calls. To Olivia, some of the calls appeared to be of a personal nature, and some were business. But one thing was certain—the Cubs were part of all of them. Olivia was happy to know that no one was looking over their shoulders and keeping track of every moment of their time. As long as the customers were being called on, regulars were getting their orders filled, and they stayed busy, she assumed all was well.

Jake summed it up: "We had a successful morning with a great sale to the senior care facility."

Now it was time for lunch, so they headed out to a great little spot he knew of, in the Lincoln Park neighborhood looking out on Lake Michigan.

Still stuffed from breakfast, Olivia ordered a small salad while Jake ordered the chef's fish special of the day.

This time the chef came out to greet him and meet the new associate. "I've known this guy for years," Chef said. She learned that the two had played on the same softball team at Millennium Park. "Hey, do you know why QAZ is such a great company? It's the kind of awesome customer service and creative solutions this guy comes up with every time. That's why I give him all my business," Chef said.

"Really? That's fantastic," Olivia answered, for the first time that day truly excited. At last. She was about to *learn something*. "Can you tell me what kind of value he delivers that would help me, as a new salesperson, earn that kind of loyalty from an account?"

That question seemed to take Chef by surprise. After a pause that lasted a few seconds more than it probably should have, he answered, almost defensively. "Well, I trust Jake. We go back a long way. He's never done me wrong. He always gives me the best quality product, fair prices, and deliveries show up like clockwork. Plus, there are times when he goes out of his way to pick up products and deliver them when the restaurant is in need. And then there's *this*," he added, gesturing around the restaurant. "You know, we see each other every few days. For lunch. And sometimes happy hour. Or even for dinner after a Cubs game!" At this, Jake and Chef bumped fists conspiratorially.

When they got back to the car, Jake was quiet for a moment or two. Then he asked Olivia just what, precisely, she thought she was doing. "What did you hope to accomplish by asking Chef to explain himself back there?"

Olivia was flummoxed. "I...I was actually moved that he trusts you with all his business, Jake. I wanted to understand your 'secret sauce.' I wanted to learn."

At this, Jake chuckled. "Well, honey, next time I'd appreciate it if you'd hold your horses just a bit, cool your heels, and ask me how it's done *after* I've finished the sales call. The last thing I need is a ride-along asking why somebody is doing business with me. The competition is always knocking at my customers' doors. They wave super discounted prices at them and make promises about additional services they can't possibly deliver. My customers can count me, they trust me, and heck, most of them are good friends. That's my secret sauce. It's not really a secret. Happy?"

That evening, after she got home and stripped off the suit that had made her feel vaguely overdressed all day long, a very discouraged Olivia reflected on her experiences. She realized that if most of the company's customers felt loyal to their salespeople because they were *friends with them*, she would have a much more difficult challenge ahead than she had anticipated when she was hired. Once she officially got her territory assignment, how was she going to build this kind of strong, enduring friendship with customers? Did potential customers have relationships with sales associates from her competition? If they trusted the people who had come before her at QAZ, would they immediately trust her? She began to worry about the challenges ahead. She started to plan how to build her own strong relationships, but also understood this was going to take some time. She hoped

Jeremy was going to be able to make a smooth transition for her to take over the territory.

Most of that week's training was just like Monday's experience, with few exceptions. On Wednesday, they were joined by a young woman who was a manufacturer's representative of fresh cut fruits. The rep referred to her products as "fruit-in-a-bucket." She gave samples to each chef and asked them to try the product. Not only did it have great fresh taste, but it was priced right, timesaving, and easy to store. By the end of the day, customers had placed orders for ten cases of the fruit-in-a-bucket, with promises for additional orders over the next few weeks. Overall, Olivia found the ride-along experience stimulating; it gave her insight into how she could bring additional value as an associate to a restaurant owner.

Friday afternoon was a crazy end of her first week out in the field. Four of Jake's customers called him with problems. The first one was missing a case of cheese and corn tortillas from his delivery, and they needed those products for the weekend. Two had received so many reservations for Saturday night that they needed additional protein items. Lastly, his good buddy Chef called to ask for help because his sous chef was ill and not able to work that evening. Like a true seasoned veteran, Jake took immediate action and headed to a big-box store for the additional products, as it was too long a drive back to the warehouse. Upon picking up the items needed for his customers, Jake and Olivia (still riding along) drove by the Mexican restaurant, dropping off the cheese and tortillas.

Then Jake went above and beyond. "Olivia, could you drop off the meat and fish to the other two restaurants? I need to go help Chef prepare for tonight's dinner rush." Olivia was astounded, but glad to help. No wonder Chef trusted Jake.

Grabbing the products, she loaded up her car and thought of this opportunity as a welcome way of paying him back for spending the week training her. Like many people, her mind wondered while she was driving. The power young people have to multitask allowed her mind to never stop working on finding better solutions. If this situation happened to her in the future, she would be able to incorporate technology to provide faster communication with the restaurant owners. She would use the big box store's app to have her order ready for pick up, or she might have the order delivered by a rideshare company. These options are readily available, and created by her generation. After all, what would Jake have done if she hadn't been around to help him out of this jam?

RAINMAKER PRINCIPLES
CHAPTER 6

- It is not the job of an experienced salesperson or a rainmaker to field train new hires. It is the job of an accomplished manager trained to grow rainmakers.

- A great lesson for millennials or a younger generation to understand is the value of great service when a customer does business with a rainmaker. This is what drives results for customer loyalty and prevents the customer from purchasing online or buying from an average salesperson for the lowest price.

- If a sales manager was a trained rainmaker coach and was doing the field training, most of the generational aha moments would have been acknowledged, discussed and memorized for future training.

7 | The Death of a Sales Dream

After a great weekend visiting friends in Southern Illinois, Olivia arrived home and began her preparation for the week ahead.

Jake had recommended that she move straight ahead to riding along with Jeremy, and she was excited. This was her chance to show Jeremy what she had learned and was capable of accomplishing in her new territory. She mapped out her plan. She would visit new prospects, make a couple of daily/weekly visits to take orders from existing customers, and try to set up a meeting with a chef/owner of a restaurant with a great concept and three locations. Her idea was to introduce Jeremy to the chef and have him offer the client a free business review.

By eleven o'clock Sunday evening she still hadn't heard from the boss, so she sent him a text to confirm the time and place of their Monday morning meeting.

"MEET AT OFFICE" came the all-caps quick reply.

Having to drive to the main facility to meet at Jeremy's office before hitting the road Monday morning was a drag. She'd have to fight Chicago traffic for nearly two hours only to turn around and head back in the opposite direction, but that was what the boss wanted. Quickly, Olivia pointed this out, but Jeremy texted back.

"HAVE EARLY WORK TO DO. NOT JUST ABOUT TAKING ONE CAR. YOU CAN ALSO PICK UP ANY LAST-MINUTE ITEMS CUSTOMERS MAY NEED"

Olivia wasn't very happy about the arrangement, especially since she couldn't imagine which items she would have to pick up. She didn't even *have* customers assigned to her yet. But, she did as she was instructed.

Once on the road together, she immediately changed her attitude. For one thing, *no sports radio*. Olivia was energized by Jeremy's positive, motivational chatter. He really believed in her and was constantly saying she was going to become a sales superstar.

They arrived at the first customer around midmorning —a three-generation family restaurant that has been a customer of the company for many years. Before getting out of the car, she pulled out her laptop to review and show Jeremy her pre-call preparation, completed the prior evening.

Being a millennial has its advantages when it comes to technology. Olivia understood how the CRM worked. She could access her customers, their purchase history, pricing, email correspondence from the previous sales rep, and various other notes. This was a great and powerful tool. Of course, all the information had to be captured and filed in the right places. Unfortunately, it seemed that everyone at their company was using it their own way—and not very consistently.

Jeremy liked what she showed him, and they went in through the kitchen entrance. He seemed to know everyone, from the dishwasher to the line chefs. He didn't speak very much Spanish, but he seemed to communicate at some level with everyone. Jeremy introduced her to the manager and soon they were connecting. She was given the nickel tour of the kitchen. From there, she did the inventory and wrote up an order for the boss to review. He made a few changes in quantities and prices, talked the manager into buying two of the weekly specials, and they were on their way to the next stop.

The rest of the first day and the next few days went rather smoothly. Olivia was feeling confident that she could do the job until their first stop on Thursday. They walked into the back door of one of the largest steakhouses in her territory, which had several locations throughout the city, to hear the general manager reject a large delivery from QAZ. He was angry and yelling at the driver when they arrived. When he saw Jeremy, he turned beet red and started in on him.

Apparently, he had been leaving Jeremy messages over the past few weeks about late deliveries and missing items. Since his old account manager had quit, he had not been happy. "My voicemails have been completely ignored!" he yelled at Jeremy. "I've decided to shop the competition and they've more than earned my business."

"I'm so sorry. I haven't been ignoring you, honestly—things have been in an uproar since we lost four reps in rapid succession," Jeremy tried to explain. "We'll fix these problems now that we're staffing up. Have you met Olivia? Let's work out some fantastic pricing that can't be beat. If you can just accept today's shipment, we can take a moment to talk. We can work this out. You've been a customer for years. Can we go inside?"

Eventually, he got the manager to agree and proceeded to work out an incredible deal for the entire chain. While Olivia stood by silently, Jeremy promised the manager that he would personally handle the entire account and not to worry about different sales people pushing them for more business. He promised to demand that the logistics manager schedule deliveries for the steakhouse the first thing every day. They ended up shaking hands and agreeing to everything, while Olivia and two other reps lost one of the largest accounts the company had, with the snap of a finger.

When they got back in the car, Olivia sat in the passenger seat in stunned, silent disbelief. Jeremy, on the other hand, was pumped that he had saved the customer and was going to grow the chain to become QAZ's largest account.

"Olivia," he said, "Grab your laptop, place the order with this new pricing, and enter the notes into the CRM. I'll provide the overrides and change the account manager's name to mine later."

Olivia was so upset she could hardly hold back the tears. This was so unfair, and so harmful to her and her fellow teammates, that she could scream.

She pushed on and their next stop was a cold call on a new restaurant with a farm-to-fork theme. Jeremy told her, "Take the lead and sell this one." He was going to stay in the car and catch up on a couple of phone calls. With the wind knocked out of her sails, Olivia proceeded to go in and meet the chef. They chatted a bit and Olivia left him with a list of their specials. Having just seen Jeremy cut her off at the knees, her heart simply wasn't in it, and she left without an order.

Getting in the car, she opened her laptop and made a few notes while setting up her next visit to the chef. Jeremy was still on the phone and signaled for her to drive on to the next stop. He spent most of the day on the phone bragging about how he handled things at the steak house, while she spent most of the day thinking about what a jerk he was being. It was a tough challenge for her to make it through the rest of the day. The saving grace or silver lining was that the bossman gave her the green light to begin working her territory on her own.

The next year-and-a-half seemed to go by like a flash to Olivia. She worked hard, established some great relationships, and was a rising star on the sales team. Olivia was making more money than she had ever dreamed possible, and it was easy for her.

The biggest challenge of her job was having to deal with Jeremy, but she could avoid him much of the time. The sales meetings became the worst part of her week, but she had enough friends on the team and together, they could handle most things he would throw at them. Besides, there was always a good time after the meetings when they would go out, have a few drinks together and have what they euphemistically called *decompression conversations* (trash talks) about Jeremy. This became the norm until the day he announced the new pay structure… and a few "minor" changes to the territories.

That was the night Olivia decided to quit and move on with her life. She needed some fresh air and a new start, without the baggage of the bossman.

RAINMAKER PRINCIPLES
CHAPTER 7

- Showing a lack of respect for your staff, peers or clients is never acceptable.

- It's not a good leadership practice to ignore other people's ideas and put your own needs first.

- Poor communication sends the wrong message to an impressionable new hire.

- When someone shows you that they excel in a skill, such as Olivia's organizational abilities or her understanding of technology, a great manager listens and learns. Encourage ideas that can be shared and will help the whole team.

- People put up with many dysfunctions of their jobs, but when you change their compensation plan, it is usually the straw that breaks the camel's back.

THE PURSUIT

8 | Little Does Kevin Know

When Kevin walked away from his sales position at QAZ Foods, he had no idea he would one day help the person who replaced him, Olivia, to reach her dream.

But first, Kevin had his own journey to complete; the quest to be a great sales manager, a maker of rainmakers.

Kevin was a likable, hard-working man who began his career in the food industry working in his family's restaurant in the Midwest. That is where he originally met Jeremy, back in the days when Jeremy was a territory salesman on the road for a hardware supply company. Stopping in the restaurant every time he came through the area, Jeremy would chat with Kevin, and they developed a nice friendship.

Kevin was a personable young man and a quiet, understated, astute listener—not the boisterous, outgoing, typical salesman personality. He wasn't outspoken, and he made decisions based on facts rather than emotions. Kevin eventually shared his desire to move out of the family business with the QAZ sales representative that called on their restaurant. After several occasions, he was ultimately introduced to a manager at QAZ foods. That's how Kevin began his career in sales. As you recall, when Jeremy decided to leave the hardware supply business, it was Kevin that introduced him to QAZ. Both were hired by the same QAZ Foods sales manager and worked together in the same district for years. Then Jeremy became Kevin's boss.

Once Jeremy became the sales manager, their interpersonal dynamics changed. Kevin didn't appreciate the way he was being treated. Their friendship took on a new dimension. Soon, things got ugly.

Kevin initially didn't want to give an exit interview to HR, because he didn't believe in stabbing a friend in the back. But he also didn't want the salespeople still at the company to be set up for failure. So, he did agree to one in the end, and he was as diplomatic but honest as he could be regarding his reasons for leaving. Still, he didn't expect much to change. In the months and years after he left, he stayed in touch with friends at QAZ and from everything he heard, he was absolutely right. Nothing changed. With Jeremy the Rock Star in charge of the sales force, nothing would *ever* change.

Kevin immediately decided to spend his first few days indulging in his favorite pastime. Fishing was the one activity that helped him clear his head and think clearly. The first day on the water helped Kevin solidify his thoughts about his future.

The first decision was easier than he thought. First, he realized that he didn't actually enjoy being a salesman. The aspects of his job he most enjoyed were helping customers solve their problems, educating them, and working with new salespeople—especially millenials— while they were in training. The writing was on the wall (or water, if you may). Kevin decided to make a radical move and replace his sales position with a job in sales management.

The second decision was much more difficult. He concluded he simply wasn't passionate about the job in food distribution he had just left. While it was scary to look at other industries because the previous two were all he had ever known, deep in his heart he knew that he was a people person and really enjoyed teaching. Kevin knew he could achieve success as a sales manager in many industries. Not knowing what he needed to learn or how he was going to gain knowledge in a new industry worried him. But it gave him great pleasure to help other people achieve success and believed that management was his calling.

He started planning his strategy to land a job in sales management via the traditional methods. He scoured the help wanted ads on LinkedIn, Monster, and other various internet sites, contacted various executive search firms, began to fill out online applications, and submitted his résumé to anyone who appeared to have a heartbeat. These activities generated some phone interviews. A few times he was asked to take online assessments. He was called in for a couple of live interviews. Kevin was even offered two jobs to start in sales, but that just wasn't what he was looking for. After the fourth month of searching, he began to doubt that he would ever achieve his goal.

One evening, he met up with some friends at a local sports bar to watch the big game. One of the guys introduced him to Terry, a buddy of his from the west coast who was a sales rep for a major automotive paint supplier. The friend was in Chicago for a conference and was an easy guy for Kevin to hold a conversation with.

They had a few similar interests: baseball, fishing, and hot cars. During their conversations, Terry learned about Kevin's desire to become a sales manager and before the night was over, he mentioned that one of his customers was looking for someone just like Kevin. It turned out that this customer recruited people by distributing a list with the description of the type of person they were looking for to all of their vendors.

Who would have thought this would be the night that changed Kevin's life forever?

Kevin received an email from Terry first thing the following morning, introducing him to the director of sales for a national auto parts distributor. Kevin immediately composed an appropriate cover letter and emailed his résumé.

From there, the process moved along at a rather quick pace. After a phone call with the director, there was a follow-up virtual interview with a branch manager. Soon after that, the company provided Kevin with a round-trip flight and overnight accommodations in Vancouver for a set of live interviews at its B.C. branch.

During his two days onsite, he interviewed and spent a great deal of time with a variety of people from various departments. After a long first day, Kevin was given login information and asked to complete an online assessment before returning the next morning. By late morning on the second day, he was given a comprehensive presentation about the company, a precise overview of the job expectations, a detailed description of the company's management training program, and a compensation review. On the drive to the airport, the director told Kevin that the team really appreciated his time and candor. They would have a meeting to review their findings and contact him within two days.

As promised, Kevin received a call from the director late the next day. The team had agreed to move forward and have him fly to Winnipeg for a final interview with the company president. And just like that, before Kevin's head stopped spinning from a fast and furious day with the head guy, he was the new British Columbia sales manager. His next stop was Sacramento, California, where he would begin his managerial training.

There, a team from Impact Sales Coach presented the "Growing Rainmakers Boot Camp" for sales managers. It was a full five days of intensive training, led by Coach Ray the Rainmaker, focused on building systems and processes and leadership training.

The coach began the week with this simple, yet powerful vision: "The job of a sales manager is not to grow sales; it is to grow rainmakers. You need to know about the products and/or services your company sells like the back of your hand, and you have to possess many other skills and traits. But the bottom line is the vision has to be about *talent development*."

The message was loud and clear. Great managers in every department need to become great coaches to tap into the power of their people.

Coach Ray's training would fill in a lot of knowledge gaps that Kevin knew nothing about.

He told the group that since the late 1990s, business coaching had gone from a nice-to-have skill to a must-have fundamental. "Strong leaders in great organizations understand today how valuable developing others has become," he said, "and organizations began adding the skill set of coaching to their job descriptions when they realized all managers need to understand employee development to compete successfully."

That first morning, Kevin learned that coaching focuses on helping other people learn in ways that let them keep growing in the future. It is based on *asking* rather than telling, on *provoking* thought rather than giving directions, and on *holding a person accountable* for his or her personal goals and commitments, not just the company's revenue targets. Broadly speaking, the purpose of coaching is to increase effectiveness, broaden thinking, identify strengths and developmental needs, and set and achieve challenging goals. Coach Ray then gave the group a copy of a handout based on a white paper as a launching pad to discuss the skills needed to coach others.

Research from the Center for Creative Leadership has boiled down the skills managers need to coach others into five categories:

Building the relationship. It's easier to learn from someone you trust. Coaches must effectively establish boundaries and build trust by being clear about the learning and development objectives they set, showing good judgment, being patient

---

and following through on any promises and agreements they make.

Providing assessment. Where are you now and where do you want to go? Helping others to gain self-awareness and insight is a key job for a coach. You provide timely feedback and help clarify the behaviors that an employee would like to change. Assessment often focuses on gaps or inconsistencies, on current performance vs. desired performance, words vs. actions and intention vs. impact.

Challenging thinking and assumptions. Thinking about thinking is an important part of the coaching process. Coaches ask open-ended questions, push for alternative solutions to problems and encourage reasonable risk-taking.

Supporting and encouraging. As partners in learning, coaches listen carefully, are open to the perspectives of others and allow employees to vent emotions without judgment. They encourage employees to make progress toward their goals, and they recognize their successes.

Driving results. What can you show for it? Effective coaching is about achieving goals. The coach helps the employee set meaningful ones and identify specific behaviors or steps for meeting them. The coach helps to clarify milestones or measures of success and holds the employee accountable for them.

Understanding that the best sales managers are actually great coaches made a lot of sense to Kevin. But he also realized, if you're going to grow a powerful sales team, you have to start with the right people—talented people who are a great fit for the company's culture, and people who resonate with the company's vision and mission.

Kevin figured with the right people on his team, coaching them to become rainmakers was going to be exactly the type of management job he had always dreamed about. But swimming around in his head were questions like, "Where do you advertise to discover these people? What does the ad look like? How do you know a superstar when you see one? And how do you get the best candidate to join your team?"

Luckily, those questions were exactly what the rest of the week would answer.

RAINMAKER PRINCIPLES
CHAPTER 8

- In work, as in life, always follow your passions.

- It's not always who you know. Sometimes it is who knows you.

- Proactive companies recruit staff through trusted advisors.

- The job of a sales manager is not making sales; it is growing rainmakers.

- Managers in the modern marketplace must have the skill set of coaching in order to develop people across generations.

- Coaching increases effectiveness, broadens thinking, and lets people focus on their individual strengths to achieve their goals.

- A manager needs to become proficient in the five categories of skills as defined by the Center for Creative Leadership.

9 | Enter the Mentor: Coach Ray the Rainmaker

Coach Ray the Rainmaker grew up in Chicago, where he started his first company before graduating from college. With a background in music and business, together with his longtime friend and business partner Ken, Ray built a very successful business. Their basic beliefs centered around offering the right products, providing great service, engaging in focused marketing, and creating all the procedures necessary to operate smoothly.

Their core philosophy was to mentor, educate, and grow the staff, because if you did that, revenue would soon follow. Even before Jim Collins wrote his book *Good to Great* at the turn of the century, they believed that you must get "the right people on the bus, the wrong people off the bus, and the right people in the right seats." After two decades following this line of thinking, the pair sold their business and Ray moved to Northern California.

There, just outside of Sacramento, he developed and launched Impact Sales Coach, a training company for all aspects of business development and sales management, centering his new consulting business around the same core philosophy. He dedicated his company's efforts to building championship teams by growing managers into coaches and growing salespeople into rainmakers.

In the weeklong training, Kevin connected to much of what Coach Ray was saying about coaching, getting the right people hired, and especially his simple formula for success:

Attitude + Skills + Activities = Success

Coach Ray the Rainmaker stressed the recipe: "It's not attitude *or* skills *or* activities alone that make a successful rainmaker. You need *all three attributes* to succeed."

Now the hard part began. Each of the workshop attendees had to define those three parts of the success formula. Each began by listing nine preeminent criteria that best defined the attitude they expected from their direct reports, attempting to identify the traits that were most important and frequently key to success in the job; in other words, which traits were nonnegotiable or must-haves. What defined the attitude necessary to achieve greatness in their department? Coach Ray provided sample lists of approximately thirty traits to get them started. They could choose from that list or create their own.

Kevin and the other sales managers in the training populated their lists differently, based on their industry. Alexia and Dan, two of the other attendees, worked in IT consulting and heavy equipment sales respectively, and Coach Ray used their table to write examples on a whiteboard and illustrate a cross-section of their thoughts:

Attitude

(See Appendix for Coach Ray's sample list)

Kevin Automobile Parts	Alexia IT Consultants	Dan Heavy Equipment
Positive— Can Do	Confident	Intense
Win-Win	Coachable	Capitalistic
Curious	Enthusiastic	Moldable
Tenacious	Flexible	Positive
Goal-Focused	Resilient	Enthusiastic
Competitive	Leadership	Motivated to Succeed
Ethical	Passionate	Energetic
Creative	Integrity	Youthful
Team Championship	Unselfish	Money-Bent

During the discussion that followed, most of the sales managers ultimately agreed that defining attitude was going to be their most difficult task. Most of them had not given a lot of thought to defining attitude when it came to a new hire.

What came to light during the next hour was that each of the people in the training had very different ideas of what makes a rainmaker's attitude. Alexia, the IT sales manager, said, "I want a staff I can train to do things my way, and people who are driven to become leaders. They have to be very giving with their time and knowledge in order to help their customers and coworkers meet their needs. They'll ignore rejection and keep driving to achieve the results they want."

Dan, the heavy equipment sales manager, on the other hand, said he was seeking "A team of upbeat, energetic people who are self-starters." Coach Ray asked what that meant. In his dynamic way, Dan answered, "I drive results by pushing for daily accountability and by holding commissions and bonus numbers in front of their noses." It seemed obvious to the workshop attendees that Dan desired a team of younger people with big dreams looking for large monetary rewards.

While Coach Ray kept writing things on the whiteboard and flip charts, it became clear relatively early that there was no right or wrong attitude for a world-class sales team.

Kevin said, "My ideal team would be made up of individuals who are focused on achieving their own dreams—salespeople who are hell-bent on being number one, while at the same time willing to help the staff around them succeed at reaching *their* goals." As Coach Ray nodded and scribbled to keep up, Kevin said *his* ideal team would use their creativity to solve customers' problems, provide solutions for their needs, and work with fellow staff members as a team. Identifying the attitude of a rainmaker or sales superstar was Kevin's intent, and it appeared that he would achieve his desired results. Many attendees felt a sense of alignment with Kevin's definitions.

Establishing the criteria that defines attitude was a challenge to the group, but they all agreed that *attitude* was the most important of the three elements (attitude, skills, and activities) that create success.

Coach Ray and the Impact Sales Coach staff repeatedly gave examples of how great attitudes had driven the highest levels of results in the shortest time with companies they had worked with through the years.

"The reality is," Coach Ray said, "that teaching or changing people's attitudes is very challenging. When you are coaching somebody to improve their attitude, you should expect incremental steps toward growth. By comparison, coaching to teach new skills and activities that people need to be successful in sales is easy. Improving those areas is a much easier task than improving attitude."

"Speaking of skills, we found that a large percentage of the sales skills needed were the same or similar for all of the companies regardless of their industries," Coach Ray stated.

Most of the managers in the workshop struggled with the belief that the skills their salespeople needed were not unique to their company or industry.

"Selling enterprise software is different. Technology is changing very quickly." Alexia asserted. And Dan crossed his arms and said, "Well try selling multimillion-dollar construction equipment that sometimes lasts fifty years." And as far as Kevin was concerned, he hadn't even started his new job yet or worked in his new industry, but he was relatively sure that selling auto parts would be different than selling nineteen varieties of fresh lettuce or four dozen different cuts of french fries.

Coach Ray smiled. That was the usual response from the attendees at rainmaker workshops. But the coaches had prepared for this part of the exercise, and it was group participation. Once the group began to hear each other's thoughts defining the necessary selling skills for their industries, they realized they were listing areas of great overlap among their various products, services, and selling processes. Ultimately, they struggled with limiting themselves to nine must-have criteria. They ended up with very similar lists of skills to define top producers in their respective fields.

Skills
(See Appendix for Coach Ray's sample list)

Kevin Automobile Parts	Alexia IT Consultants	Dan Heavy Equipment
Closing—Asking for the Business	Pre-Call Preparation including Research	Time and Territory Management
Questioning and Listening	Communication, Internal and External	Product and Industry Knowledge
Critical Thinking	Follow Through	Stress Management
Differentiation	Time Management	Quoting
Oral and Written Communication	Objection Management	Communication, Internal and External
Follow Through	Relationship Building	Referral Generation
Product Knowledge	Public Speaking	Value Add
Time Management	Asking Questions	Follow up
Prospecting	Systems Knowledge	Technology

Kevin, Alexia, and Dan were amazed. The commonalities across their industries were remarkable when they focused on the *skills* needed in a top producer, especially when they were limited to just a handful of critical criteria and skills. Most of the managers wanted to include additional criteria, but they understood that it was essential to limit the list to the most important. Coach Ray told them they were building a tool, and they had to keep it tight if they were going to be able to use this tool effectively to help find and grow the best sales talent.

Prior to outlining the final criterion in the three-part recipe for attitude/skills/activities, Kevin asked Coach Ray if this was the same thing as goal setting. This prompted an informal discussion that lasted through lunch about goals, targets, accountability, and strategic planning—a sure sign the group was engaged and on fire.

Once the group got back from their meal, Coach Ray the Rainmaker got them focused on the project at hand, promising to cover these subjects in more detail on day two of the workshop.

Defining the ideal rainmaker's traits/criteria for activities was easy, except that once again, each manager was tempted to put every possible activity on his or her list. This desire is not unusual. In reality, most salespeople need to do more than just nine activities to be successful at their job. Coach Ray reminded the group several times that they should focus on the traits they believed were *most important* and *frequent* for success in the job.

When all was said and done, this was what the group and Ray wrote on the whiteboard and flip charts.

Activities

(See Appendix for Coach Ray's sample list)

Kevin Automobile Parts	Alexia IT Consultants	Dan Heavy Equipment
Cold Calling	Pre-Call Preparation	Asking for Referrals
Follow up	Business Process Reviews	Goal Development, Focus and Achievement
Learning New Products/ Techniques	Asking for Testimonials	Opportunity Assessment
Promotion Participation	Social Network for Personal Marketing	Product Demonstrations
CRM usage	Org. Chart Capture	Profit Analysis
Budgets	Team Selling	Competitive Analysis
Reports and Paperwork	Internal Communication	Relationship Stuff with Customers
Pricing to Win	Strategic Planning	Trade Shows
Use Sales Tools	Creative Ideas	Networking Events

The criteria defining the top activities turned out to be a very diverse list. It didn't seem possible that these definitions were all talking about what is expected from people in the same position.

Through this structured exercise, the group of sales managers grew to understand that, while *attitude* was biased to reflect the organizational culture, and *skills* were fairly similar for many sales positions, *activities* were true differentiators. Activities were genuinely diverse and based on the selling processes of different companies in different industries.

Now that each manager had a list of criteria that defined his or her success model, Coach Ray instructed the group to transfer their lists into a spreadsheet, creating a tool that he called the eMatrix (an employee matrix).

"This tool," Coach Ray said, "is considered the nucleus of the Impact Sales Coach Model and we use it to grow rainmakers. From this point, you will use the eMatrix tool to define everything, from ranking your current staff to discovering new top talent. You'll use it to develop written job expectations, provide subjects to focus your sales meetings, improve communication, develop individual growth plans, help to measure results, and hold people accountable, just to name a few. The eMatrix is as unique as your business and your team, but it's grounded in the best practices of coaching. Yes, we use it for growing sales people into rainmakers, but it can be adapted for growing people in operations, logistics, management, sports, or even raising children.

"While working with one of our clients who hired us to help facilitate a succession plan, they were struggling to transition their clients to the next generation of business. They hired a young woman who had a diverse work history including working for one of the leading technology companies. Using the eMatrix process, we were able to define not only her strengths and weaknesses, but the senior management's as well. Based on the results, we were able to structure systems and processes that met the needs of the senior management's way of doing business and integrated the fresh ideas of the new generation. This had a profound effect on providing solutions utilizing the strengths of all generations within the company. It provided an understanding that all generations had something to offer in growing the business—from the younger generation's command of technology and innovative ways of conducting business to the senior management's experience and relationships," Coach Ray added.

With that said, Coach Ray stressed this point: "All twenty-seven areas are important and will be used in a variety of ways that will be explained over the next few days. Please keep in mind that you will not be using all twenty-seven criteria at one time. You will be asked to decide on a smaller, focused group of criteria to be used to individually grow, train, develop, and educate your people, what areas you need to focus on during sales meetings, what are the must-have traits to develop a recruitment list, and many other uses. The full eMatrix will only be used to gain an overview of your expectations and to open communication of expectations with your staff."

The ranking system is simple, consisting of four numbers and four colors:

1 = Not meeting your expectations—Red
2 = Sometimes meeting your expectations—Yellow

3 = Meeting your expectations—Green

4 = Exceeding your expectations—Blue

Once the numbers are plugged into the eMatrix, the colors of each cell will change. The visual effect will provide an immediate depiction of what areas your people are or are not meeting.

Having given deep thought to every part of the day's training, Kevin submitted the example of the eMatrix he planned to use. He would rank the staff he was about to inherit once he met them all. He would also give the staff an opportunity to rank themselves in each of the twenty-seven areas. This would quickly facilitate an overview of his expectations and open the lines of clear communication.

(See Appendix for Coach Ray's eMatrix samples)

RAINMAKER PRINCIPLES
CHAPTER 9

- Bridge the generation gap by incorporating the strengths of everyone in your training, on your team, in your industry, and through the wisdom of others.

- The simple formula for success in sales, business, and life is Attitude + Skills + Activities = Success. Once these three areas are defined, your success will be directly attached to your level of achievement in each.

- Attitude is the most important part of success in the world of rainmakers.

- Defining the traits or criteria of the three-part recipe for success establishes the basic performance expectations for each individual on your team. Take your time to decide on these criteria, because they will become a very important piece of the puzzle you will use to grow rainmakers.

- The eMatrix tool provides the focus for group training, identifies individual performance improvement areas, improves communication, helps with accountability, and is used to create recruiting tools and more.

10 | Key Number One— Recruit and Hire the Best

Day two of the Growing Rainmakers training for managers began with a forty-thousand-foot view of the Five Key Result Areas used to build championship teams of rainmakers.

BUILDING A WORLD CLASS SALES ORGANIZATION

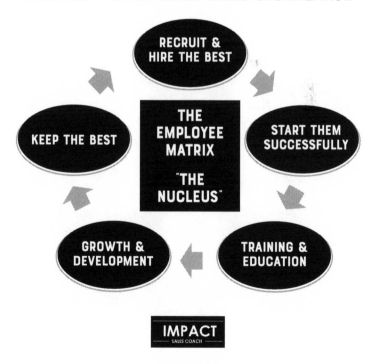

1. Recruit and Hire the Best
2. Get Them Started Successfully
3. Training and Education
4. Growth and Development
5. Keep the Best

Today the group was nodding their heads. "Hiring top talent is the first step to creating a successful team," Coach Ray was saying. "It doesn't matter what industry or what department you're managing. The only thing that matters is to start with top talent. Now, who here has a great track record of making good hires on a regular basis?"

He looked around the room. No hands went up. Kevin had never hired anyone at all. It became rapidly obvious that finding top sales talent in any business isn't easy.

"OK, well, that's a sign. So, let me tell you definitively what you already know. You can't hire top talent effectively or efficiently with ads on various internet job sites or through newspaper ads. Given the large number of applicants that wash through those channels, it's extremely difficult to discover the real person that way," Coach Ray said.

Alexia raised her hand. "We tend to go to staffing companies. What about them?"

"Well, that's one way to go," Coach Ray answered, "But they have drawbacks of a different nature. Many times, staffing companies can source top talent, but they are very expensive. Since recruiters earn commission on their placements, once they place someone, it's not unusual for recruiters to stay in touch with that person for future opportunities. After all, that is how they earn their money."

Kevin was genuinely startled. He had never experienced this type of practice before, but soon learned from spontaneous group discussion that, while not all recruiters operate this way, enough do, so that several boot camp participants had personal stories to confirm the existence of the practice. They had all lost relatively fresh hires within two or three years—to the very same recruiter who had sent the new hire their way in the first place.

As an alternative to recruiting firms, Coach Ray recommended a complete, start-to-finish business procedure.

"The long-term hiring success and retention rate is much higher when a manager follows this type of plan," Coach Ray said, "and even when a position is not currently available, top sales managers spend the energy to develop a full recruiting hopper of qualified potential hires. It's just like collegiate and professional sports; recruiting is not a sometime job for a manager. It's an all-the-time job."

The next exercise was for the managers to build a Profile Form.

"Look at your eMatrix," Coach Ray said, "and choose twelve must-have traits to consider putting on this list. These traits will describe the type of new recruits you are looking for. Yesterday you all agreed that attitude is the most important of the three attributes that define a rainmaker's success, so based on that, pull six criteria from your list of attitude criteria. Mix them with a few of your must-have skills and finally, if the position requires special experience, desires or education criteria, complete the list with those. This will give you a Recruiting Profile with a maximum of twelve requirements."

At the end of the exercise, Kevin had developed the following. As he did so, he thought back to the kinds of generic help-wanted ads he'd seen on sites like Craigslist through the years. He immediately saw the difference as the Profile Form developed.

RECRUITING PROFILE

(See Appendix for Coach Ray's profile form and samples)

Manager:	Kevin S.......	Email:	Kevin.s@pbp.com
Position:	Outside Sales	Phone:	222-555-1212

These are the attributes or character traits that represent the chemistry of the most successful outside sales and business development people at our distributorship. If you know people who fit some or all of these traits, please forward their information to me. I will, in turn, introduce them to an awesome opportunity for a new career.

1. Ethical—Shows uncompromised morals
2. Creative—New and original ideas
3. Positive—Can-do attitude
4. Sets Goals—Works to achieve them
5. Competitive—Yet still a team player
6. Curious—Interested in learning everything
7. Critical thinker—Driven to find solutions
8. Car aficionado—Knows and works on cars
9. Great communicator—Well spoken
10. Outgoing—Likes to meet new people, cold-calling
11. Computer-savvy—Uses as part of everyday life
12. Participates in promotions—Upselling experience

Recruit's Name:		Email: Phone:	
Referral Source:		Email: Phone:	

When all of the managers had finished their profile drafts, Coach Ray said, "Now when you need to add a great person to your team, you can focus on building relationships with potential employees. The profile form is a tool that allows you to communicate to vendors, partners, friends, and even coworkers to help you find the *kind of person* who fits your needs. They may not necessarily have X years of progressively responsible experience selling in your industry, but they'll have what you know is important in your organization—the right attitude, skills, and abilities—because you've identified those and you've said those are what you need. When you are constantly working to fill the hopper with people you know—people who have the top success traits to be successful under your coaching—you now have the ability to look everywhere, not just in a help wanted ad in your own industry. You'll be able to find the 'right people for the right seats of your bus.'"

Coach Ray was on fire.

"Recruiting is only half of the job of getting the right person on your team," he told the sales managers. "The hiring process itself is the other part of the equation. You need an integrated system to uncover the real person inside of a candidate. The process will also allow strong candidates to understand the culture of your company, understand the opportunity, and make them sincerely want to be the person you hire. A system is much more effective than a couple of ad-hoc interviews. Hiring requires a fully prepared hiring committee armed with a procedure. You need quality interview questions, systematic follow-up based on the candidates' answers, and an organized debriefing process."

And then he was off, outlining all the details of exactly such a system. The details and questions and answers lasted for hours.

The last hour before lunch, the group participated in interview role practice.

In the mock-hiring exercise, Kevin, Alexia, and Dan were chosen as the hiring team, while one of the other attendees, Angi, played the potential candidate. Coach Ray gave each of the hiring managers a different set of questions, and one at a time, they asked questions of the candidate. The rest of the group acted as outside observers, taking copious notes.

The interview progressed from Kevin asking the basic broad-based background questions to Alexia digging deeper with more applicable sales solution questions. She was asking for specific times when Angi had used various types of solution selling in the past. After a few questions and listening to her high-level responses, Dan jumped in and asked if he could join Alexia with follow-up. He proceeded to dig even deeper, not accepting the candidate's initial answers. Showing very well-developed listening skills, he used what Coach Ray had taught in the morning session, probing for little things that didn't add up. He asked Angi how she did things, what actions she had taken in the past, what help she might need in the future, what tools she used, how negotiations had proceeded, and timelines, all in an effort to pull out the granular details and facts of the situation. Building on

Dan's questions, Alexia also asked about future situations and how the candidate would approach similar situations with new clients but under different circumstances.

Through this exercise, the group observed the benefit of asking pre-determined questions and demonstrating great listening skills. This enabled them to uncover the full truth about the past, as well as digging for details about a candidate's orientation toward the future.

"Capturing detailed notes is essential for all interviewers," Coach Ray emphasized at the end of the exercise, "because those notes will be used in the team debrief before you decide on making an offer to a candidate. Now, before we break for lunch, I want to emphasize that in addition to the interview process, hiring the right person requires a good pre-employment screening assessment. Of course, your hiring committee needs a comprehensive understanding of what the results from these assessments mean in real-life situations. We'll talk about that in this workshop eventually. It's also covered extensively in your playbook. But when you come back, we're going to move on to the onboarding process."

RAINMAKER PRINCIPLES
CHAPTER 10

- The five keys to building a championship team of rainmakers are:
  - *Recruit and Hire the Best*
  - Get Them Started Successfully
  - Training and Education
  - Growth and Development
  - Keep the Best

- Recruiting is not a part-time job for managers; it needs your full-time attention.

- Creating and distributing a profile for every position you are responsible for is essential for recruiting successfully.

- Recruiting top talent is one thing; Hiring top talent is the other half of the equation.

- Implement an integrated hiring process designed to uncover the true identity of the candidate through coordinated questioning, and use multiple staff participation.

11 | Key Number Two— Get Them Started Successfully

The group's lunch was filled with excited chatter; they knew they were learning something special.

Kevin talked about how he had been recruited for his job and told the others about the hiring process. "It was grueling, but fair," he concluded. Then the group started discussing Coach Ray's methodical recruiting process for hiring top talent with their own previous experiences, both hiring and being hired, and they were especially intrigued by the idea of looking for new sales staff through their extended professional networks like vendors and contractors; that was an approach that simply made sense.

The afternoon session couldn't start soon enough.

After they reassembled, Coach Ray asked the group to describe what the typical first day looked like for a new hire in their company.

The overwhelming majority of their answers sounded similar. They all began the same way: "Filling out paperwork in Human Resources." At most of the companies represented, this process seemed to take between a few hours to a full day. Some new hires spent time with HR or an administrative assistant showing the new employee around the office and introducing him or her to a plethora of new faces. In some cases, the new hires went from HR directly to the product training class; on a few occasions they actually got to tag along on sales calls.

Coach Ray the Rainmaker next spoke about research on how to improve retention starting on day one. "People are efficient evaluators," he told his aspiring sales manager superstars. "They form impressions based on existing biases. And their biases start the moment they walk in your door. In psychology, a first impression begins when a person encounters another person and forms an initial mental image, which can greatly influence how this person is treated and viewed in many contexts of everyday life from that moment forward. With this in mind, I am going to make a strong recommendation. *Only* start a new hire when you are available to spend at least a full day with that person. You will never have another chance to make up for a new hire's first day if you aren't there to welcome him or her to the team personally."

Coach Ray had additional tips and advice to streamline day one. "Most of HR paperwork can either be completed in advance of starting the job, and some of it could perhaps wait a few days. And we all know the basics," Coach Ray said, "But you'd be surprised how often we don't get those right. Often a new hire gets to the job site and nothing is ready for him or her. No computer, email, training itinerary, updated job description. Sometimes they don't get business cards for two months—they walk into accounts and hand them their manager's card with a name crossed out and their own written in smudged ink. They get no structured briefing on customers or competitors, let alone the essentials like where the restrooms are located. Besides the managers being available to introduce the new hire, it is essential to assign new hires a buddy to help with questions for the first week or two."

As the group was laughing at the examples being laid out before them, they couldn't help but nod in agreement that this didn't position new hires to start successfully. It was exactly what the experience looked like in their own companies.

Closing this part of the discussion, one of Ray's assistant coaches said new sales employees usually wonder if they have made a mistake by starting with a new company. After all, they are made to feel uncomfortable from the first day. They don't know anyone. They are stuck doing paperwork for hours. Nothing seems ready for them to start. They don't know the plan or expectations. There may be a lack of support at home and many times there is intense pressure to start earning commissions from spouses, kids, or other family members. "How can they succeed when every message they're getting screams uncertainty and desperation?" she concluded.

Coach Ray the Rainmaker related a story about one top-producing salesperson who had resigned from a client he had coached. It turned out that one of their competitors had made promises for more base pay and a fantastic territory for her to work. Within the first thirty days, many people question their decision to have left their previous position and start with a new company. In this case, the coach suggested that the sales manager call the rainmaker at her new office after the first few days. The manager was coached to let her know how much they missed her already and promised to keep her desk open for her as long as they could in case she changed her mind. He also opened the door for a conversation over coffee in place of an exit interview. She was open to that idea. When they met, the sales manager listened attentively to all of her challenges—those that had occurred while she had worked for him as well as those she was experiencing at the new company.

The following weekend, the two ended up going to a basketball game together with their spouses, as they often had in the past. And by the end of the evening, she asked the manager if the offer to come back was still available. "While it doesn't always work out this well," Coach Ray told the group, "if you ever find yourself in a spot when you really want to bring someone back that just quit, keep this story in mind. Put your ego in a drawer, listen, and keep the door open. Heck, it can't hurt."

Through this collaborative effort, they created a checklist of must-have items before a new hire started their first day. The list included personalized business cards, their own business email address, a computer, cell phone, company logo wear, and a ready-to-go workspace or office. The group also felt it was important to have all necessary software and apps available, including the company's chosen CRM system, access to the company's proprietary shared drives and a staff directory. The group agreed these things should be waiting for new hires at their assigned desks the moment they arrived on their first day. They also decided that, based on each company's business rules, the outside business development people should be provided with a company credit card, details on expense suggestions and limits, and a territory map including the contact information of their existing customers. In addition, every new hire should be assigned a training buddy to help with anything from finding their way around the physical buildings to understanding how internal things got done quickly and efficiently.

The group of sales managers also loved Coach Ray's suggestion to send a gift basket welcoming the new rainmaker's spouse to their new family. They all agreed that this one simple move was a great way to help build support at home.

The remainder of the afternoon was dedicated to beginning the process of creating a complete training procedure for the sales managers based on their companies' unique needs. This was a major undertaking and would require a collaboration with other staff members from each of their companies, including everyone from administration to senior executives. The coach's goal was to gain a commitment from the managers to create a ninety-day training plan. It was the consensus of the Impact Sales Coach team that with proper ninety-day onboarding training, a great recruit should be able to engage with a customer or prospect and have a meaningful business conversation. "A new hire has to be able to carry out the vision of the leadership team," Coach Ray said. "For those things to happen, a new hire has to know the vision, experience it throughout the company, believe in the vision and communicate it in a way the customer needs to hear it." Everybody in the training group, from Kevin to Alexia and Dan, nodded in agreement.

Coach Ray returned to his whiteboard and began to talk and write. "The ninety-day learning plan needs to include everything. Details need to be established that include how long each subject will be taught, who is involved in the teaching, where the training will take place—either physically or online through eLearning— and there needs to be a quiz or some other sort of assessment at the end of each thirty-day period. This is the absolute minimum you need to cover."

- Product knowledge
- Industry knowledge and trends
- Company history
- Sales training
- Sales procedures
- Operational execution
- Past successes and failures
- Customer analysis
- Customer needs
- Customer pains and fears
- Differentiations between our company and our competitors
- Pricing to win

- How to use various software programs
- Delivery and logistics
- Travel and entertainment policies and guidelines
- How sales targets and goals are created and measured
- Full implementation and use of the CRM
- The list goes on...what else?

"When you assess your new hires every thirty days," Coach Ray said, "the quiz can absolutely be open book. Because your employee will always have access to his or her resources to look things up if need be. But your new hire should achieve 90 percent correct answers in order to be allowed to continue. While this may seem harsh, it is a realistic goal if you hired correctly. This way of training is fair to everyone; it provides the education to grow rainmakers and follows the philosophy of hiring slow and firing fast. There's no sense stringing along a bad hire and hoping to turn that person into a good hire. It almost never works out."

It was a long day. As the group worked on creating their individual onboarding plans, they came up with more questions than answers, but the managers were fired up to learn more. When they were given a homework assignment to complete that evening, no one seemed to mind. Creating a comprehensive table of contents for their ninety-day training plan was the perfect conclusion to a great day.

RAINMAKER PRINCIPLES
CHAPTER 11

- The five keys to building a championship team of rainmakers are:
  - Recruit and Hire the Best
  - *Get Them Started Successfully*
  - Training and Education
  - Growth and Development
  - Keep the Best

- Managers should never start a new hire unless they are able to spend at least the first full day with that person.

- Have everything ready and waiting for new hires on their first day, including all necessary equipment, email address and business cards.

- It's a good idea to assign a "training buddy" to help new hires become acclimated to their new world.

- Have an onboarding plan for every position in your firm.

- The longest time in a manager's life is between the time they realize a person is not working out and the time that they terminate that person. Always remember to *hire slow and fire fast.*

12 | Key Number Three— Training and Education

As the group of managers began to assemble the next morning, they were asked to display their outlines for their ninety-day training plans around the room. Everybody was a bit bleary-eyed and it was obvious some of them had stayed up into the wee hours to complete their assignments; they were double-fisting coffee.

While everybody got properly caffeinated, they walked around and discussed some of the various ideas created by others. A group question-and-answer period followed. This collaborative effort became a powerful driver, and every manager took additional notes as they came up with additional ideas to improve their initial training plans.

It became very clear to all that they should be able to train the right person to begin paying for their seat on the bus by the end of their first quarter with the firm. This didn't mean that they would be fully trained as top sales professionals within three months; rather, they should be able to make meetings and have meaningful business conversations at the end of the initial ninety days.

Coach Ray guided the conversation from new-hire training to what type of ongoing training is needed to grow rainmakers. "In our fast-changing world, it is challenging to keep current with everything," he said. "What methods have you utilized in the past to keep your people informed?"

The group began a brief roundtable covering both their successes and failures. Dan said, "Salespeople typically feel they know everything, not just about what they are selling, but everything. What I often hear before and during training sessions is they just want to get back out to the customers. While they are sitting in training meetings, the competition is talking to and stealing their customers."

Coach Ray the Rainmaker showed empathy. "That's not unusual. But next time you hear that, ask them this: wouldn't their customers be more loyal if the salespeople were able to deliver higher levels of additional value on every visit? In today's highly competitive market place, customer *satisfaction* is nothing. Customer *loyalty* is everything. Rainmakers need to do more than just build relationships. They must stay ahead of industry changes, understand marketplace trends, adapt to improvements made by their counterparts, and deal with new competition from pricing models found on the internet and the ever-evolving world of apps. Even if our salespeople don't understand or want to keep up with all the external threats to their success, it's our job as their managers to keep them informed and to give them everything they need to deal with those threats."

"Ongoing and continual education of the new products and services your company has created, changed, or improved upon should be scheduled on a regular basis," Coach Ray said. "How often this training is provided depends strictly on the speed that your industry moves, the complexity of your services, and your firm's innovation schedule. I would imagine Alexia's firm will need this kind of education monthly or bimonthly, while Dan's can probably do it on an annual basis, because IT moves at the speed of light and heavy equipment sometimes doesn't change more than once a decade. It varies. Understanding how new product releases can help solve your client's problems or provide services that improve performance is only part of the story, though."

"Let's look at Kevin's world, for example. Sales in the highly competitive B2B world happen less than half the time based on price-to-value ratio, brand loyalty, product difference, or service. Over 50 percent of customers in that world say that having meaningful business conversations with a rainmaker provides the value they seek when they decide whom to buy from. So, for Kevin, when he's training his sales professionals, he needs to be sure they can *challenge the customer's way of thinking* and *educate them on what they have learned* so they can create those meaningful business conversations. That will be the focus of his ongoing training and education. For the rest of you, it will be something else. The art of creating rainmakers isn't one-size-fits all. It's definitely driven by the industry, by the market, by the niche, by the product, by the price, by the service, and by a host of other factors. That's what I'm here to help you figure out this week."

The managers split up into two work groups, this time with the challenge of discovering what type of subjects they needed to teach their salespeople in an effort to provide necessary insights their customers were seeking.

As they talked, ideas moved from traditional training about what products they sold to how their staff sold. The coach leading one of the groups asked Alexia how her staff went to market as an IT consultant. She said that most of the time, they responded to requests for proposals and participated in the bid process. She admitted that this method provided them with a very low closing ratio and ever-shrinking margins.

One of the other managers asked about meaningful business conversations: were those part of her sales process? If the sales representative could offer interesting and worthwhile perspectives on the marketplace, that might be one step toward leading the customer to position the RFP in their favor. This one simple idea opened a flow of ideas that got the discussion rolling for a good long time.

Kevin chimed in with some thoughts from his days back in the food service industry, telling a story of how he had once helped a restaurant owner by helping her understand alternative ways to deal with changing federal and state compensation laws. While that was far outside the scope of french fries, produce, and meat, he had been able to educate the owner in advance of potential problems she was about to face, and that ability to establish trust with the business owner had gone a long way toward establishing a trusting, problem-solving relationship. Then another manager shared that he was able to provide introductions to a consultant that had helped his client secure a state-run grant program to offset training costs at his own business.

In a second group, the coach asked, "What value do your sales staff bring to prospects or clients beyond superior products and service?" Dan couldn't hold back his enthusiasm. He shared that his team had recently begun to discuss new ideas with prospects based on new issues in their industry—alternative construction solutions and how to avoid potential environmental and regulatory land mines. They had taken the new approach, acting as consultants rather than simply being sellers of heavy equipment. Digging deep to uncover the pains experienced by the prospect or customer and really gaining an understanding of what they fear moving forward, uncovering the challenges ahead, had helped his best salespeople get ahead of the game.

Following a new Ready–Set–Go methodology he learned previously, Dan explained that his salespeople were now able to identify why certain initiatives would succeed or fail.

These Ready conversations were not very easy to have, but from previous coaching experience, Dan said he had learned that the customer wants to learn. "Good or bad, Coach Ray is right. Customers want to learn before they spend the resources to begin an expensive purchase. They look at—and value—suppliers that find new ways to provide efficiencies, hire top talent, retain top producers, grow revenues, infiltrate new markets, get a different perspective on their industry, and to avoid taking unnecessary risks."

Coach Ray looked so pleased he was about ready to burst. He couldn't have said it better himself. With Dan's unbidden testimonial underlining everything he'd said, he sent the groups back to work on their own assignments. They needed to figure out how their own salespeople could become experts who would bring knowledge and consulting value to the business owners and accounts they called on.

As the day progressed, the groups reassembled and discussed their findings. It became quite obvious that this was a new way to think about their jobs—and not just to grow sales numbers. In order to compete, they had to become subject matter experts on training. *What* to train on, *who* to best provide this education, *when*, and *how*.

In the afternoon, Coach Ray the Rainmaker talked with Dan in front of the group about how his team had built a Question Guide to offer their sales team a concise way to learn what to ask, as well as how to dig deeper into the answers they heard in an effort to provide true consulting services. Of course, once the Question Guide was built, they never stopped editing it, adding new relative issues and sharing the responses heard. (*See Appendix for sample Question Guide*)

"There are many tools of the trade that most companies don't provide for their new salespeople; even fewer that help their top performers stay on top of their game," Coach Ray told the group. "All sales tools need to be continually updated, improved upon, and practiced professionally, in-house, not in front of the customer. Just imagine if you had top-quality marketing and presentation materials that connected the dots between the marketing and sales department. Dan and his company are ahead on this. What would be the ROI if you had a Question Guide that could be used for the new hire training? It could continue to help the entire staff for role practice, pre-call preparation and to gain a better understanding of your customer's needs or problems. You can find more information about many of the resources we implement in your Coach's Playbook. We'll touch on all of these in the next few days, and of course, for the next year, I'm yours. Just pick up the phone and I'll answer any questions you have."

Coach Ray meant it, too. There was too much to learn about creating rainmakers to fit into just five days, he'd told the group over and over again, and he'd be at their disposal through email or telephone for the next twelve months if they needed clarification or reminders.

A brown bag Lunch and Learn session was on the menu for day three. As the group began to dig in, a number of short videos were projected onto the big screen. These consisted of a variety of vignettes of people discussing the selling methodology they were using in their practice. This led to the managers in the group adding their own experiences and conversations revealing the pros and cons of each method they have used.

The common thread for the most respected methods centered on the theme of putting the customers' needs to succeed in front of the rainmakers need to sell. Coach

Ray the Rainmaker added that top rainmakers take control of the sale by building trust when engaging in meaningful business conversations throughout the customer's organization.

Coach Ray said, "Rainmakers share their knowledge and ask questions to understand the customers' needs and challenges completely. Then, and only then, do they present a well-designed 'Anchored Presentation.' It is anchored to the prospect or customer's motivators. It always contains a quantified business case that includes backup validation. And it demonstrates win-win solutions."

Alexia asked a question: "How do CRMs fit in?"

"Ah," Coach Ray answered. "The proper use of a CRM (Client Relationship Management) tool is a weeklong training all on its own. There are many fine programs on the market. And when they are used correctly, they can be powerful. But honestly, in a lot of organizations, a CRM can be the number one software expense that does not provide an ROI and quite frankly, it is *not* used correctly by many salespeople. Rightly or wrongly, most salespeople and sales leadership believe a CRM is just a means of Big Brother watching. That thought process should be far from the truth, but it is partially correct. If you know what you want out of the program, decide how you are going to use it. Then train everyone to use it in the same fashion, and it will help everyone to form new positive sales habits. As a sales manager, you will have transparency into your team's activities because the CRM tells a story by capturing notes, emails, and past history—allowing you to schedule the next action steps all in one place. It provides you with the platform to collaborate with your people, and it becomes an indispensable tool. In addition to all of the above, a CRM helps you stay in touch with contacts as they switch jobs, moving from one employer to the next. You are able to keep the background history that may have taken years to discover. And finally, you can use it to hold everybody to the same standards of accountability."

Alexia, as an IT solutions manager, looked thoughtful and nodded, making extensive notes. Coach Ray could see her gears turning. *Probably thinking about how to create engaging, non-intimidating CRM trainings for salespeople,* he thought.

The last few hours that afternoon were spent with the managers each giving a ten-minute presentation explaining the advantage of doing business with their company to the group. Each presenter was judged on his or her presentation skills, communication style, and content. This exercise was followed with a short but powerful seminar on how to improve their presentations entitled Spark the Enthusiasm.

Overnight, the group again had homework: make changes to their presentations based on the seminar and get up again the next morning, this time with the goal of *wowing* the audience.

RAINMAKER PRINCIPLES
CHAPTER 12

- The five keys to building a championship team of rainmakers are:
  - Recruit and Hire the Best
  - Get Them Started Successfully
  - *Training and Education*
  - Growth and Development
  - Keep the Best

- Have a written ninety-day training process for all new hires, include a thirty-day quiz at the end of each month.

- Customer satisfaction is worthless, but customer loyalty is priceless; train people to become trusted advisors.

- Rainmakers stay ahead of industry changes, marketplace trends, improvements made to products/services or alternative solutions provided by competitors.

- Customers are always searching to learn more, understand more, and are constantly looking for suppliers that can teach them and their people. They want to do business with rainmakers.

- Two of the most important rainmaker sales tools are Question Guides and Success Story Guides—See Appendix for Coach Ray's samples

- Client Relationship Management (CRM) systems help drive powerful results, but the key is to have them set up and used correctly from the moment they are implemented.

13 | Key Number Four — Growth and Development

Day four dawned bright and clear. The group reassembled, grabbed their coffee, and dove into their revamped presentations. The presentations truly took on new sparks of enthusiasm by using techniques that Coach Ray had covered in the seminar the day before. Things like *setting the course*, articulating what *benefits* the audience was going to receive, and *encouraging interactive participation* throughout each presentation made a tremendous difference. The most noticeable verbiage changes, though, were the use of *the seven magic words* (see appendix for Coach Ray's list) shared by the coach the previous day. Last and certainly not least, each presenter had *solid closing statements* that established action items for both the audience and presenter. Everybody was energized by the revamped presentations, and congratulations flowed with third and fourth cups of coffee.

Certainly, the managers were all moved by the fact that the right training and education could provide their team with drastically improved presentation results.

Most successful operations departments have well-established procedures for every task needed to conduct business. With that in mind, the coach asked the managers what type of systems and processes they had in place to help their salespeople succeed.

Surprisingly, a few had systems designed for qualifying leads and even activities to begin prospecting. Three of the managers had territory management systems, and all had at least one sales ordering process.

There was, however, an obvious lack of consistency when it came to providing business rules for every aspect of business development. As history has shown, sales seem to present a black hole when it comes to standardized procedures. It is a mystery how companies allow individuals to use their own ideas, do their own thing, *do what you have always done*, when it comes to selling.

The group spent the next few hours developing a list of systems and processes needed to create a *Rainmaker's Playbook* for all of the managers' teams. The list included email templates, scripts for inbound and outbound voicemail, dialogues for conversation flow, question guides, objection management formulas, negotiation techniques, success story manuscripts and other deliverables for each manager to develop and share with his or her team, creating an outline to work from.

Using this type of organized approach for sales takes the mystery out of the equation. Now activities and results could be measured, results analyzed, and changes made to improve. Using standardized methodology and procedures would certainly help to continually grow and develop the manager's people into rainmakers.

Kevin, as well as most of the group, seemed to understand the importance of each of the systems and processes, but was finding it difficult to stay focused on the project at hand. It wasn't that the managers didn't believe that having a *Rainmaker's Playbook* was important, or that it would make a huge difference to their team. It was just very challenging because most of the sales managers didn't possess this type of detail-oriented thinking skill (which is something most of their personality assessments would have shown, had they gone over the results as a group).

As the group discussed how to get the systems and processes documented and assembled into playbooks, it became obvious that this would and should be a work in progress in every organization.

Dan said, "Bits and pieces of our system and process development were used as topics and training during our sales meetings the whole time we've been developing them. In my experience, this isn't a playbook or manual that *one* person has to sit down and create before sharing it with the team. In fact, they all agreed that having some solid guidelines was very valuable, but getting everybody to work on it together as a living, breathing document was actually priceless. They're out there on the front lines every day. They know as much as I do about our systems and processes and what works. Creating this procedures documentation together also helps to build team buy-in."

One of the more seasoned sales managers thought it would be a good idea to use the eMatrix to identify leaders who could help drive the various topics that need improvement based on individual scores. "If one team member is strong at asking questions and others are weak in that area, the stronger team member could develop and lead exercises to build a collaborative question guide. If another staff member who scores high in teamwork could lead a role-practice session, that could be used to help people listen better and answer questions without hesitation. And so on."

Kevin thought that was a great idea and filed it away to use in his new job.

Next, using the eMatrix tool as the nucleus once again, the coaches provided a template to develop and improve a PIP (performance improvement plan) that they would customize to help each of their people grow into rainmakers. This individualized approach is designed for their people to work on a few specific competencies. Together with their manager, it helps them with quarterly growth, and it provides an accountability program at the same time. A performance improvement plan that is based on identifying three traits out of the twenty-seven criteria each quarter based on Attitude, Skills and Activities, made the managers feel encouraged. They could provide the personalized mentorship that would provide growth and development of their people.

The purpose is to help a rainmaker understand which dimensions could use improvement, and the resulting plan was to be discussed with the staff member to open new lines of communication. "After all, since we all agreed that the job of a sales manager is to grow your people, not to make sales, this one tool is going to be a major key to your ultimate success as a manager," Coach Ray told the group. "When you base performance discussions around this tool, it will keep expectations centered around how the two of you together can work on improving. You will also want to explore what other resources might be available to help. You'll use this tool to set milestones you expect staff to meet throughout the quarter. Yes, this tool will take a great amount of time and work to create for each employee, because each rainmaker is an individual with unique talents and challenges. You'll need to define lesson plans and coach each team member because no two people are exactly the same. But if you want to grow a championship team of rainmakers, it will be worth it."

Coach Ray and the other Impact Sales Coaches offered many resources they have used to help individual development using the PIP as a platform:

- Individual coaching sessions
- Individual reading
- Webinars
- Seminars
- Group education sessions taking place during sales meetings
- Manager-led training
- Staff-led training
- Outside training
- Vendor training
- Blogs, vlogs and podcasts
- TED Talks and other online videos
- Books, articles and other reading material

"At the end of the quarter, based on the goals outlined in the individualized performance improvement plan, both the manager and employee will do a self-evaluation, then will meet one-to-one to discuss accomplishments or failures, communicate about the next steps, and decide on the next quarter's focus," Coach Ray said, wrapping up the morning's session.

After some lighthearted discussions at lunch, which were sorely needed after the intensity of the morning, Coach Ray brought the group back together and mentioned one additional bonus of the growth and accountability program: It provides a communication tool for the managers to share their work with their bosses and HR. As a matter of fact, many CEOs find so much value in having their sales managers using the eMatrix system that they implement it throughout the rest of the organization.

The afternoon session continued to focus on growth and development, but the subject matter began with a seminar on time management.

"With all of the new expectations we're introducing and the new manager/coach activities you're going to have to squeeze into your existing workload, we know you're going to have to find a new way to tame the time monster," Coach Ray said. "Don't worry. We feel your pain."

The time management session lasted a full afternoon. The sales managers learned fundamental skills, from blocking time to email and phone call management to learning to prioritize. Kevin found the most valuable lesson of the day was a simple use of the alphabet.

He'd always struggled with getting things done. And sometimes he found himself up late at night sending emails, even if they were fairly noncritical. After Coach Ray and the rest of the Impact Sales Coach team were finished with the time management portion of day four, Kevin never made that mistake again. He learned to rank and rerank his To-Do list constantly according to the following scale, understanding nobody would ever cross every item off the list:

- A (priority)
- B (important)
- C (nice to do)
- D (delegate)
- E (eliminate)

Kevin learned that rainmakers focus on their *A* list first and foremost, then on eliminating items on their *E* list, followed by the *B* and *C* ranking, and finally they delegate the *D* list. Putting as much importance to their Not-To-Do list as their To-Do list is something Jim Collins said he noticed about the best leaders in his book *Good to Great*. Another eye-opener for Kevin was learning to define and schedule the three *most important activities* he should do *every day* to add value to the company's success. Kevin found that identifying the *C*, *D*, and *E* time bandits was a key that would help him stay on track.

"In the end," Coach Ray explained, "there is no time management without goal setting. You see, people do things for their own reasons. It is the managers' duty to help their people identify their own personal goals. Help them achieve their dreams and they will walk on water for you."

Dan, who had been involved with Coach Ray when he was a sales pro shouted out enthusiastically that he agreed wholeheartedly. It turned out that he had created his goals when he was just starting out, and his manager at that time and the coach had helped him succeed. He eventually hit every one of his goals, including donating blood twenty-four times. Dan said he had earned and saved enough bonus money to reach another one of his goals: he took his wife on a Mediterranean cruise. Eventually Dan was promoted to a position as the Midwest Regional Sales Manager. Dan said his goals were the driving forces behind his professional and personal successes. He realized early on that his financial goals had to be in line with the company's sales targets, but he also noted that his boss always checked in on his personal goals too. He received great support to help achieve all his written goals.

"Goal setting is only useful if individuals capture their dreams in writing and develop a plan that will drive them to achieve their goals," Coach Ray said, "And as Dan just pointed out, for this to take place, these must be meaningful, personal goals—goals that the person is passionate about and that their spouse or significant other and manager supports.

"See, Kevin, I told you we'd talk about goal setting eventually. Once personal goals are set, another very important tool that helps to achieve individual and group growth is *strategic planning*. And I'm not referring to the overall strategic *business* plan for the sales and marketing departments. I'm talking about an *individual rainmaker's* strategic territory or revenue plan. This is a plan the staff member develops collaboratively with you—the sales manager. It's a plan they envision as their best course of action to achieve their own goals and the company's targets. We'll talk about developing those as well. Where is it?"

"In the *Playbook!*", the group said in unison.

Yes, growing rainmakers was not an easy job, but not an impossible job, either.

The last hour of that afternoon was spent reviewing the Sales and Marketing template for the rainmaker's territory. The energy being generated by the managers was incredible. Time seemed to fly as they shared their wisdom from past experience, asked open-ended questions, and expressed new ideas. When the end of the day came, they were all very relieved to hear the announcement of no homework that evening.

RAINMAKER PRINCIPLES
CHAPTER 13

- The five keys to building a championship team of rainmakers are:
  - Recruit and Hire the Best
  - Get Them Started Successfully
  - Training and Education
  - *Growth and Development*
  - Keep the Best

- The *Coach's Playbook* is a resource to help a manager with the systems and processes to build a championship team. It is filled with the management systems and processes that focuses on the eMatrix and the five keys.

- The *Rainmaker's Playbook* provides an organized approach for sales or business development and takes the mystery out of the equation.

- Managers and their teams should develop a list of all the systems, processes, sales tools and methodologies to begin creating their own *Rainmaker's Playbooks*. This needs to be a living, breathing book that continues to grow, improve and adapt to changes.

- Group and individual growth and development plans are both important to grow rainmakers.

- Time is our most important resource. We can't
  buy more time; we can only manage it more
  efficiently.

  - Learn to prioritize and delegate.

  - Schedule blocks of time for daily tasks.

  - Define the three most important tasks you
    do for your company and schedule time for
    them.

  - There is no time management without goal
    setting.

14 | Key Number Five— Keeping the Rainmakers

Finally, it was Friday.

Kevin, Alexia, and Dan gathered around the giant coffee pot for their final day of sales manager boot camp. Discussion centered around how each manager was going to incorporate what they had learned during the week into their team.

After a half-hour or so, Alexia the IT manager said she felt confident about being able to recruit, hire, and train the right person to become a rainmaker. What bothered her, though, was the fact that her industry was notorious for recruiting the best people from the competition. It had been her experience that when one or more of her people started to be successful, someone from the competition would come along and recruit them from under her nose. "Even if I build a championship team," she asked the group, "How do I keep it together?"

Yes, growing rainmakers and building a team was one thing, but keeping them was another.

Coach Ray nodded. "Basketball legend Michael Jordan once said, 'Talent wins games, but teamwork and intelligence wins championships.'"

Kevin jumped in and stated the obvious: "My company doesn't have the resources to pay for Michael Jordan's salary."

Everybody laughed.

"Well, of course not," Coach Ray answered. "But you'd be surprised. Compensation is only part of the reason that people leave their jobs. Let's talk about that, though. Here, I've got a handout."

And indeed he did.

"Look at this. In a 2014 study by *Forbes* magazine, this writer, Jacquelyn Smith, uncovered that most workers who are dissatisfied with their job overall are most likely to find new employment. While 66 percent of those workers cited concerns over salary, nearly the exact same number—65 percent—said *they don't feel valued*. Some other reasons her research had identified were poor work/life balance, poor opinions about their boss's performance, overlooked for a promotion, not receiving a base pay increase, poor benefits and a lack of recognition. Now look at the next study. *Harvard Business Review* says the reason top sales professionals left their jobs were: Number one, respect; number two, recognition; and *number five*, compensation. So, we may tell ourselves people leave over money, but that's just not the case. There are a lot of things we can do to keep people around that have nothing to do with money.

"To turbocharge rainmaker retention, sales managers need to know the hearts and minds of their people," Coach Ray concluded.

All the sales managers kept flipping back and forth through the pages of their handouts as if they expected to find something...*different*...in the pages.

One of the other coaches broke the silence by pointing out the previous afternoon's discussion: "Dan's company did that very thing years ago when it helped him with personal goal setting and alignment with the company sales targets. And they didn't stop there. They also helped him achieve his goals by encouraging him to achieve milestones, held him accountable and rewarded his accomplishments. Right, Dan?"

Dan totally agreed.

Coach Ray picked up the thread. "While goal setting is a great starting point, it is necessary to build great relationships with each member of your team as individuals. Building trust through caring, giving recognition, and showing respect to your people is where it begins. You need to be able to have open, nonthreatening conversations about your people's challenges, dreams, and their passions. Positions and job expectations need to be molded to satisfy a person's life interests. Sometimes, you need to make adjustments and remove an employee's dislikes. Listening, really listening to learn about your people, will show the respect that most people, especially rainmakers, are seeking. And respecting rainmakers' personal achievements can also be shown by including them in decision-making activities. Some of your people may want to be part of the new hire team, strategic planning at the highest levels, or involved in product and service development. What are some other ways to show them respect? Let's talk about that."

The next exercise for the group was focused on building a list of ideas that would show respect to their top producers.

Recognizing the accomplishments of rainmakers seemed to be a simple task. Most of the managers had experience with bonus programs, competitive sales challenges for high-end prizes, various types of high achievement clubs and award dinners.

One of the coaches asked if anyone had ever experienced *too much* recognition by a manager before.

Alexia was busting out of her seat to tell a story she had witnessed at a previous company. It wasn't so much about overly recognizing a rainmaker's success as it was not knowing what your people care about.

"One of the bosses invited the team to join him outside in the parking lot one afternoon during the weekly sales meeting for their company," she told the group, more animated than they had seen her all week. From her body language and descriptive gestures they could practically see the facility and feel the blazing sun on the blacktop.

"When the whole team was assembled, he announced 'the number one salesman for the month was now going to have the front parking stall.' As a side note, this building's parking was at a premium. Right by the front door, there was a new sign erected in the first spot that read 'Salesman of the Month.' Then around the corner came his assistant driving a beautiful red

Jaguar convertible and the assistant parked in that front parking spot.

"Next, the sales manager made the announcement that he and the big boss had decided that the top producer of the month needed a new ride to show his success. Their 'top dog' no longer needed to drive around in an old beater. With that, the entire staff knew who the Salesman of the Month was. He was a family man in his mid-forties who joined the team about six months prior and had been number one since his second month at the firm. He drove an old turquoise Geo Tracker that must have had a couple of hundred thousand miles on it. A few of us joked it must have been held together with love, bubblegum, and duct tape. That car was often towed behind his family camper. One thing was sure; the sales manager and the big boss would never be caught dead in it. The sales manager always insisted on taking his own car when the two of them visited prospects or when they went to lunch together. When the sales manager tossed the Salesman of the Month the keys to the shiny new Jag, the salesman tossed them right back. He looked the manager right in the eye and said, "I don't need a car. I have one. I also *have* three brilliant children who need books, clothes, food, school supplies, health insurance and a lot of money for their future college tuition. You don't even know who I am, who my family is, or what we are about. Let me tell you, in my life, the last thing I need is a temperamental, expensive, foreign car. I don't need a sports car to make sales. I just need better pay for my results." With that, this guy turned on his heels and walked over to his love-gum-and-duct-tape Geo Tracker and left for the weekend.

"A few months later, this salesman broke the company's all-time monthly sales record, and that was the day he quit. Eventually he started his own consulting business where he shared his knowledge and experiences to help others achieve success. I never, ever forgot that man's face the day he threw those keys back at the sales manager. It taught me that not everybody wants the same things, and if you get it wrong early, you may never earn the chance to get it right."

Alexia's story really drove home the idea that building a relationship with salespeople as individuals is absolutely necessary to build and retain top talent. A manager has to earn the trust of his or her people. Knowing what drives people is the key to being able to recognize their achievements. That insight drives many leaders to understand friendship is a key to teamwork.

President Abraham Lincoln once said, *"If you would win a man to your cause, first convince him that you are his sincere friend."*

To reinforce the importance of truly connecting with each of their salespeople, Coach Ray passed out a laminated card to each manager with the quote stated above on one side and these words on the other:

"A good boss makes his people realize they have more ability than they think they have so that they consistently do better work than they thought they could."
CHARLES ERWIN WILSON

Another good quote on this subject comes from John Maxwell in his book *The 360° Leader*: "People can usually trace their successes and failures to the relationships in their lives. The same is true when it comes to leadership. The quality of the relationship you have with your leader will impact your success or failure."

For the remainder of the morning, the managers reviewed a case study published by Heidi K. Gardner, a professor of organizational behavior at Harvard Business School, examining the effects of pay on retaining employees. "While making employees more desirable to competitors may seem counterintuitive, there is ample evidence that salary is just one part of the toolkit managers need to retain their best and brightest." That said, pay does matter beyond people just needing a paycheck, but because pay is a point of perceived fairness. Everyone agreed that fairness is what matters most to people. So, ultimately, a successful manager/coach needs to figure out how to consistently treat everyone fairly.

RAINMAKER PRINCIPLES

CHAPTER 14

- The five keys to building a championship team of rainmakers are:
  - Recruit and Hire the Best
  - Get Them Started Successfully
  - Training and Education
  - Growth and Development
  - *Keep the Best*

- Letting rainmakers know that they are valued by the company and their clients is key to retention.

- Managers need to build strong relationships with their team members. Build trust through:
  - Listening and really caring
  - Providing private and public recognition
  - Showing respect at all times

- It's healthy for a manager to have open and nonthreatening conversations with your people about their challenges, dreams and passions.

- There is a great saying often attributed to Zig Ziglar: "They don't care how much you know until they know how much you care."

15 | The Buck Stops Here

A lively discussion at lunch stirred many ideas about the pros and cons of various compensation programs that the managers had either personally experienced or heard about from their staff members. Many of the stories shared, naturally, were from the perspective of being in the trenches. As salespeople, the managers agreed universally that they had often been confused regarding how much commission they were being paid. Many of them felt that they hadn't been on the same side with the payroll department and had many challenges verifying their payroll in a timely fashion. Others talked about what they had encountered dealing with pay practices from a manager's perspective.

One consistent theme that seemed to run rampant was the lack of support from upper management to keep up with salary increases being offered by competitors for their people. And worse than that was the difficult task of keeping costs down *and* keeping employees when business was slow. Often, they were expected to support alternative compensation plans that lowered baseline pay with the promise of more commission during slow economic times or industry lulls. They all agreed it wasn't always the rainmaker's fault for business being slow; sometimes it was simply the ebbs and flows of the economy or struggles within the industry. On occasion it was other departments' failures to produce positive results or at times it was the lack of new product development.

Kevin opened up and shared a personal story about a time when he was in food sales and had been subjected to *both* a cut in commissions *and* a change in territory at the same time. "My boss said, 'I never change a man's rice bowl, but this time it is necessary and don't worry, it will be good for everyone in the long run,'" Kevin remembered, shaking his head. "That was actually the last straw. I quit the following month."

The group laughed, but in a sympathetic way— Kevin had been quite open with the group about his experiences with Jeremy throughout the week of sales manager training. By now they all recognized another Jeremy story when they heard it. In fact, a couple of the other sales managers had started to say, "Don't be a Jeremy!" to each other in the same way kids might say "Don't be a jerk!"

The final few hours of the workshop were spent reviewing and discussing their companies' current compensation plans. The entire group agreed that, beyond the paycheck, the better and more complete the benefit packages, the more positive the culture. Alexia mentioned that it had been her experience that when she had casual conversations with friends and family about her benefit plan, they always commented on how lucky she was and how they wished their company was so caring for their staff and families.

Coach Ray asked the group to create and refine another list to reflect the top benefits each manager could suggest to their respective companies. The items that stood out on this list were:

- Retirement plans to which the company made substantial contributions (not just small matching contributions)
- Profit-sharing plans
- Healthcare covering both the employee and their family
- Healthcare plans that include dental and eye care
- Flexible hours so employees could have a better work/life balance
- Paid personal days rather than a set weekly vacation plan
- Tuition assistance
- Supplemental life and health insurance
- Specialized training
- Implementation of quarterly reviews aimed to improve accountability along with annual baseline pay reviews based on merit increases to reward top performers

The room was filled with sales managers, so inevitably they asked the coaching team to provide some ideas and details on designing top-quality sales commission and bonus programs. All the managers wanted to know the coaches' secrets to the most effective compensation that would help them hire and keep rainmakers on a championship sales team.

"How did I know you'd ask me that?" Coach Ray smiled. "In today's economy, there are six rules for fair compensation that will keep you competitive, no matter what kind of incentive program you establish," he said.

Then he reached for a final handout:

1. **Provide a solid baseline salary**, not one that makes sales staff too comfortable but fair pay for them to perform all the tasks required of them while providing consistent base income. Forget about the old commission-only model, it doesn't work in the twenty-first century, and stop thinking you can start a rainmaker on a good base salary and then lower it as they start to produce. It just doesn't work.

2. **Once the compensation plan has been established, write it down** and don't change it. (If you really must change it, then consider offering to grandfather in employees moving forward. Perhaps you can give them a choice, but realize that it may conflict with any new employee's perceptions and loyalties).

3. **Use bonus programs as short-term incentives** to drive specific results such as moving new products, services, or excess inventory, or dramatically increasing activities. Distribute bonuses publicly during sales meetings to generate excitement. (A suggestion was made by Alexia to use bonus programs as incentive for other positions, motivating employees from other departments

to meet and exceed their goals and give everyone the opportunity to increase their earnings).

4. **Keep commission and bonus programs simple** so employees understand what they need to do in order to be rewarded. The test for a good incentive part of your compensation plan is that it consists of no more than two to four performance factors, and all employees can accurately explain the plan in the time it takes to ride an elevator ten floors.

5. **Incentives based on the team's overall results are OK** as a small part of the incentive program but most of this type of pay should be based on individual performance. Team-based bonus programs have been known to cause resentment and backfire on a regular basis unless the team is structured from the start to share (as you will see below).

6. **Pay the employees the baseline salary portion of their compensation bi-monthly or every two weeks.** Pay the incentive portion monthly or quarterly which are both more motivating than annually. In addition, always write the incentive check separately from the salary portion of the compensation.

Coach Ray then distributed several spreadsheets and other resources on a thumb drive. These provided interactive ways for the managers to design creative incentive compensation plans.

All the proposals were geared to hire and retain top talent, but one program stood out from the rest. The coaching staff explained that they had collaborated with one of their regular coaching clients, a wealth management firm for months creating this compensation program.

The first step was to design a sales team that would enable advisors at every level to be better at their jobs and more productive. They also wanted to reduce the turnover of entry level staff, work as a team with their clients and prospects, improve hunting and farming for sales, and provide more opportunities for the entire team to grow. The result was a design that consisted of two associates, two leads, and one senior sales position. Once this five-member *Pentagon Team* was complete, onboarding new hires and talent development became easier. Educating, training, and mentoring became part of the normal workload for everyone. And everyone on the team shared in the success of every new customer and additional business from their existing clients.

PENTAGON TEAM STRUCTURE

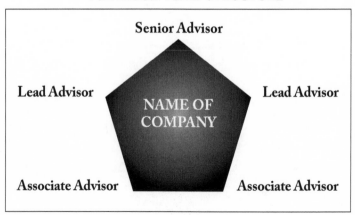

Senior Advisor

Lead Advisor

Lead Advisor

NAME OF COMPANY

Associate Advisor

Associate Advisor

On the Pentagon Team, the person who brings in a new account is considered the rainmaker, even though other members of the team usually helped to close the deal. With this team design in place, the organization created an incentive plan to reward the team for delivering the results their clients were looking to accomplish.

The first success driver was new customer acquisition. The second was to encourage great customer service so the team could ensure client retention. The third was to provide a long-term solution that would keep the team together. This was accomplished by determining the lifetime value of the customer and what percentage the company could pay as commission or success fee. Based on a formula that considered the previous history of customer turnover and typical revenue volume, Coach Ray's team and their client had determined a structure that could be paid quarterly over an extended period. This incentive plan essentially acted as an annuity for the team members and kept paying them as long they were still employed.

"You can imagine how hard it would be for someone to walk away from three to five years' worth of quarterly commissions," Coach Ray explained, "and how difficult it would be for a competitor to compete for any employee using this incentive and commission model. Who's going to leave this client of ours when all of their sales team employees are still being paid commissions for the *lifetime value of their customers*?"

The managers couldn't believe he'd held out all week on them before revealing this plan. This alone was worth the cost (and time) of the entire training, even though they'd learned so much already.

"In this compensation and incentive structure, each member of the team receives a piece of the success fee based on his or her position on the team. Plus, the rainmaker is also paid in addition to his or her position on the team. It's a complex program to establish initially. But once it's designed, I promise you, it's a lot easier to communicate to the staff than it sounds, and it's an excellent reason to continue providing outstanding customer service to existing accounts as well as to keep working on establishing new ones," Coach Ray said.

"After it was launched at our client's company," Coach Ray said, "the financial department kept track of everything on a lengthy spreadsheet. After the first quarter, once the theory was proven to work, the company commissioned a dashboard to be built into their CRM that reflected accurate, real-time results of commissions earned on each team member's CRM homepage. Talk about providing incentive—this was a work of art. Alexia asked Coach Ray if he'd mind speaking with her about the CRM customization after the workshop; he was thrilled by her interest.

As the workshop closed, the overall feeling of the group was energizing. While many had started this process believing they were enrolled to participate in a management boot camp, by the conclusion, everyone believed they had experienced a forward-thinking, innovative approach to coaching.

Based on the long goodbyes, exchanges of business cards, LinkedIn connections, and other friendly leave-takings, it appeared that the group of sales managers would stay in touch with the ISC coaches and continue to share ideas and knowledge long after the workshop had ended.

Growing rainmakers was going to be fun and rewarding.

RAINMAKER PRINCIPLES
CHAPTER 15

- Compensation is a major influence for the people who accept your job offers. Once they are members of the team, do not change the program if you desire to keep them.

- In today's modern marketplace a person's base pay initially reflects their value to join the company.

- Beyond base pay the more complete the benefit package, the more positive the culture, the better the reflection of how the company values its employees.

- Be open to develop alternative designs for sales teams that will better drive the results you seek to accomplish. These may include new hires, associates, lead sales staff and rainmakers. Creative team compensation, team collaboration, and inter-team competition are encouraged and generate powerful results.

- Here are some compensation guidelines:
  - Once set, do not change it.
  - Make it simple to understand and track.
  - Use it to drive sales results—base it on gross profit.

- Pay it monthly, in currency only.

- Establish bonus programs for every department. Use these to drive specific goals, make them flexible to be changed monthly or quarterly, and consider making them into mini-games. Beyond currency, use other types of rewards. Have fun with them!

- It is also good to implement individual and team bonus plans.

16 | Meeting the Troops

With a weekend to digest everything he'd learned, Kevin arrived at his new office just as the morning warehouse shift was assembling.

The branch manager had arrived an hour before the staff began to show up. He had hung up a map showing Kevin the territories that his staff was currently covering and a few areas that needed additional coverage.

As they reviewed it together, the branch manager suggested Kevin should consider a new hire or two to fill the gaps. Next, they took a walk around the warehouse together. The branch manager made some brief introductions, explained the overview of the operation, and in general discussed how the inside group worked with the sales staff.

When Kevin got back to his office, he immediately sat down and began making notes to capture what he had learned so far and prepare for his first sales meeting with his own staff.

As the team assembled in the small conference room, Kevin greeted each of them with a firm handshake and pleasant hello. There were four men and one woman on his Vancouver sales team. Most of the meeting was spent with the individual team members sharing their personal history, business background, experience with working at the company and giving a historic overview of their territory. Kevin appreciated them sharing the information with him and informed them that he would be setting up a private meeting with each of them to review their individual client bases, territory targets, and strategic plans in more detail.

Kevin shared his personal and sales background with the team in as much detail as they had shared with him. He spent a limited amount of time telling them about his early sales career compared with his goal to become a sales manager and how he had prepared for his new role. "While I didn't come from this industry," Kevin said to his new staff, "I want you to know I plan to help each of you grow, improve, and reach your own personal income goals. For myself, my plans include immersing myself in this industry, learning the parts, learning the applications, and spending ample amounts of time with all of you out on the road. There's no substitute for going into each of your accounts with you to learn about your day-to-day world and your customers."

Kevin hoped this would be a solid start toward building trust and a relationship with them and their customers. Kevin's hope was that as he discovered what made each of them successful, he could then share it with the others to mimic the masters.

After a short question and answer period, he shared as much as he could within limited time from the previous week's boot camp. He told them about the ISC model and that they could expect to see and collaborate on a lot of tools, systems, and processes, including a new approach to hiring, different ways to support the sales funnel and pipeline, and new sales tools. The main coaching concept he shared was Coach Ray's simple formula:

Attitude + Skills + Activities = Success

He then reviewed the eMatrix and explained how this tool was going to help them communicate with each other while identifying and quantifying the abilities of the team. Finally, Kevin sketched out a diagram of the 5 Keys to building a World-Class Sales Team and explained how the individual keys all stemmed from the eMatrix. The concept immediately seemed to resonate with the group. Kevin promised them that together they were the core of this team, that new hires would only help to make it stronger and he would help them become rainmakers.

The process began immediately. Kevin distributed the individual ranking form for the team to fill out about themselves as a baseline. This form had nine criteria to define *attitude*, nine criteria for *skills*, and nine for *activities*, all of which he had identified when designing his eMatrix during his manager training. The form included a column listing the criteria, one that spelled out the specific definitions of the criteria and one that they would use to rank themselves.

"For now, I would ask you to honestly rank yourselves on each of these criteria this way: one–not meeting the expectations, two–sometimes meeting the expectations, three–meeting the expectations, or four–exceeding the expectations," Kevin said. "You don't have to do it this minute, but I'd like you each to bring this completed sheet to our first one-to-one meeting with each other.

Just be frank. Right now, for each of the items, are you exceeding expectations, meeting expectations, sometimes meeting expectations, or failing to meet expectations per these definitions? That will give us a starting point from which to begin our work together. Think of me as a coach. It's my job to help you get better. So, if you aren't meeting expectations, that's not only OK, that's a good thing—it gives us something to work on together."

Kevin turned his attention to the next task. "Now, this request is easier. We have two territories that will need coverage soon and I will be hiring two salespeople. There will be a substantial referral bonus for anybody who recommends somebody who works out. If one of you introduces a candidate to me, and I hire that person, if he or she makes it through six weeks of training and still has the job in six months, there will be a *juicy* incentive. Here's the list of twelve must-have traits for a new person to be considered for a position on our team. What do you think?"

The list had been taken from his criteria that was used to define success, except for someone being a *car aficionado* and being *outgoing* (liking to meet new people and cold-calling). Everybody agreed the list looked like somebody who'd be a great rainmaker for the company.

The remainder of the meeting, Kevin spent asking the team to share the top questions they would ask a customer to help uncover problems they might have experienced from their delivery service.

After a few minutes, it became apparent to him that the team had little experience uncovering pains that the customer has, therefore unable to provide a solution. His quick analysis was that this team was product-driven; Kevin quickly understood why the owner referred to his sales team as *beer salesmen*—he meant they simply gathered the orders. The current sales process was to walk into a customer's business, look around, take a quick inventory, and write up whatever items were low or out-of-stock. The owner and Kevin desired the sales team to become farmers and hunters. Farmers figure out how to grow customers to purchase and possibly stock more product lines than they currently buy, while hunters look to open new accounts and add new revenue to their book of business. In short, they desired a team full of rainmakers.

Kevin had his work cut out for him. There would be training aplenty in the year ahead.

With the introductory meeting behind him, Kevin spent the rest of the week getting familiar with the nuances of the branch office and created a monthly schedule as a guideline for himself to follow, leveraging the time-management skills Coach Ray had taught.

Kevin sent out his first official email to the team advising them of his schedule plans:

To: ABC Auto Parts Sales Team
From: Kevin the Rainmaker
Re: Schedule

Thank you all for the warm welcome. I wanted to let you know my standing schedule for the week, beginning now and always subject to change depending on emerging conditions.

- 7:00 a.m. on Mondays, our team will have a mandatory hour-long team huddle (onsite here at the branch or virtually from offsite if you are visiting customers on a given Monday). The focus for the team huddle is to discuss what is new in each team member's pipeline, to learn what help is needed to close any pending deals, and to review last week's closed opportunities.

- The rest of Monday I will be reviewing individual accounts, pricing changes and individual team tasks to complete for the week ahead, but will be in the office should you need me. Individual account reviews will consist of a combination of calling clients and using the CRM to understand how I might be able to add value to a rainmaker's actions.

- Late on Monday there is a mandatory weekly nationwide manager meeting.

- Tuesday, Wednesday and Friday I will be with individual reps in the field (one full day on the road with one rainmaker at a time) meeting with customers, cold calling, marketing, strategic planning and engaging in one-to-one coaching.

- Thursday morning is the weekly sales meeting from 8:00 a.m. sharp to 11:00 a.m., in person. No excuses. The doors lock at 8:00, so don't be late.

- Thursday afternoon is open for various other management duties plus our one-to-one PIP (personal improvement plan) meetings.

- Before and after hours are unstructured; I'm here early and I stay late. My door is always open.

Spending time in the seat next to the individuals on the team was the most valuable thing in Kevin's mind to achieve his own goals: growing the individuals and reaching his regions' sales targets. Therefore, he designed his plan with at least 60 percent of his week devoted to being with his salespeople.

While Kevin didn't share the agenda of the sales meetings at this point, behind the scenes he mapped out how he was going to approach them.

He planned the focus to be on growth, development, and education the first, third and fourth week of the month. The activities for these meetings would be a combination of working together as a team to build sales tools, role practicing on how to use these tools, strategic development/planning for each territory, new product introductions, product reviews, marketing information, competitive analysis, etc. This would involve various leaders from the company who work both inside and outside of the sales department, various manufacturers' representatives, actual customers and, on occasion, guest speakers or sales trainers.

The sales meeting held in the second week of each month would be the *only* one that would include reviewing the team sales/activity targets versus the budget, individual goal achievement against the milestones established, individual recognition for achievements, and adjusting activities and strategies as needed. With the plan in place and shared with the team, Kevin couldn't wait to get started.

RAINMAKER PRINCIPLES
CHAPTER 16

- Communicating your vision as a leader is the most important first step.

- Once the criteria for the eMatrix is defined, it's easy to have individuals rank themselves, thus opening up communication with the manager.

- Distributing the recruitment form sets the stage for the team to understand what the manager's *must-have* traits are for their own positions.

- Written communication to confirm your verbal message and to share specific activities show powerful leadership.

- Declaring yourself a *rainmaker coach* and leading by example sets the bar for your followers to strive for and ultimately achieve.

PART IV

CLIMAX AND AFTERMATH

17 | Enter Kevin, the New Rainmaker Coach

Kevin's first two years in Vancouver were awesome. His weeks were filled with the excitement of learning a new industry, working through the challenges of being a leader from the middle of an organization, and growing salespeople into rainmakers.

Outside of work, he was in awe of the sheer beauty of the landscape in British Columbia. On the weekends, he indulged in his passion for fishing—and not just any fishing: going after large salmon with light tackle was more fun than he ever imagined.

Yes, life was amazing for Kevin until the offsite strategic planning meeting prior to his third year.

The three-day retreat began with the review of top-line results and profitability for every manager's territory. Kevin received praise from senior management for building a great culture within every branch in his territory, for showing steady sales increases (top-line growth from the team) and for his progress of growing a few of the average sales reps into rainmakers. The only blemish on his record was that his margins were weakening by a few points and that a very small portion of the staff were responsible for 80 percent of the revenue.

He was asked to prepare a response to deliver the next morning to answer the following three questions:

1. What challenges are you facing that eroded the profit margins to the lowest level of any other territory?
2. Why are you holding onto staff who are obviously underdelivering and underperforming?
3. What solutions are you considering that will solve these issues?

Just before the break that morning, upper management rolled out their sales targets for all the territories. Kevin, along with all the other managers, almost passed out.

The boss was looking for a double-double: double-digit growth in both sales and margins. Over lunch, the shock wore off and the managers began the process of creating ideas and solutions to achieve the desired results.

After working through the afternoon, dinner, and most of the night, morning came early for Kevin. As the leadership group gathered for the day, the owner welcomed them with a pledge to support them in any way they needed to achieve the new targets. He was a tough businessman, showed a deep passion for being the best, and was a good soul. His speech was sincere and very motivating; the company wasn't setting these targets arbitrarily. They were necessary for strategic growth that would help build an additional plant and allow the company to expand its reach into an entirely new category and geography, potentially increasing global market share by up to 30 percent within five years. This was followed by the individual managers presenting their answers to the challenges that were pointed out in the public review and their ideas for solutions.

Kevin was last to speak. He identified that his margins were being squeezed by a new competitor offering prices so low that they were just buying the business. Their impact was mostly within a heavily populated, city-center area. This was also the area of his weakest sales staff. The solution he presented was to rewrite the traits of his most successful rainmakers and edit his *must-have list* used to identify new hires. He would actively recruit, hire, and train one or two new staff members to immediately replace the poor performers. He also thought it would be a good idea to realign the city territories so that his current successful rainmakers could handle some of the load. His ride-along time would be dedicated to coaching the staff when calling on these city-center customers that they had been losing to price. And the team would focus their meetings on learning to better communicate the value proposition to these customers.

The other members in the meeting applauded Kevin. Various questions were asked, and suggestions were made. In the next few hours, the group combined ideas from all the territory managers and developed a plan to roll out their double-double initiative. They all committed to upgrading their staff. They would try to transfer good people to other departments where they were better fits or introduce them to new opportunities when that was better for the company. They all committed to spending more time in the field with the staff, helping them connect the customers to their value offers and coaching them all to improve. On the last evening, with their strategic plan in place, the group enjoyed an evening dining together and socializing afterwards for cocktails out on the patio.

It was during this celebration after dinner that Kevin noticed that his server seemed to have many of the traits listed on his recruiting list. He was having a scotch with one of the guys and asked him for his opinion.

After observing her interacting with customers around the patio for a few minutes, they agreed that she fit the criteria, except they didn't know about two key areas; did she have a passion for cars? And did she have the personality to grind it out when sales were tough?

"Say, you wouldn't happen to have a favorite car, would you?" Kevin asked the server the next time she came by to see if their group needed anything.

Her eyes seemed to brighten and a big smile came across her face. "Yes, I do. A 1969 Chevy Camaro LM1 350-cubic-inch small-block rated at 255 horsepower with a Muncie four-speed," she answered, not skipping a beat as she gathered six empty glasses and nodded at three people around the table indicating they'd like refills.

"Wow. Why that car?" asked Kevin.

"Because when I was young, I helped my dad work on one," said Olivia. "He's a great mechanic, and I skinned more than a couple of knuckles while working beside him as a kid. That car was amazing. He taught me everything about it from the tires to the trim. It put out ten foot-pounds more torque than the L30 that it replaced. That car was a serious feat of engineering. Also, it was just plain gorgeous. Darned salt on the roads in the Midwest finally got it, though. Are you still working on your drink?"

"Have you ever done body work on cars?" asked Kevin.

"Not back then, but I did some welding in high school, believe it or not, and body work is one of the many things I would love to try someday," said Olivia.

"What are you doing serving drinks when you could build a career and earn great money in sales in the automobile industry?" asked another manager.

"Sorry guys, I am yakking too much," said Olivia as she placed the final empty on her serving tray. "I need to get over there, order your refills while the bartender has a minute, and help those other customers, but I'll be back in just a few with those new drinks. Catch you in just a couple!"

RAINMAKER PRINCIPLES
CHAPTER 17

- Following your passion can lead to a happy life when there is a great work/life balance attached to it.

- Well-structured offsite planning meetings that allow time to recognize individual successes, build internal teams, present various challenges, encourage showing respect to others while collaborating to create solutions and drive initiatives...are priceless.

- Once again, we have learned that recruiting is an *all-the-time* thing for a successful manager. You can find a potential rainmaker anywhere, at any time and working in any industry.

18 Rebirth of a Sales Dream

Olivia came back to their table within a few minutes, set down the new drinks, apologized for her abruptness earlier, and introduced herself by name.

Kevin asked, "Why is someone with your knowledge and abilities working at a bar and grill?"

She briefly ran through her story, including college and her brief-but-abandoned stint in sales.

"I had to put my dream on hold," said Olivia.

"You mean the car?" asked Kevin.

"No, actually, my dream to be a great saleswoman," said Olivia. "I was so excited when I started that job. I wanted to be the person who makes it rain money. That probably sounds silly."

"It doesn't sound silly at all," said Kevin.

When she had quit her sales job back at QAZ in Chicago, Olivia was *done*. She'd happily handed over her territory to poor Earl, knowing he'd do a fine job taking care of the customers she'd established working relationships with. She really cared about those guys, but the prospect of working for Jeremy for a decade (or four) had started to give her stabbing pains in the stomach every Sunday night. Her friends and family hated seeing her miserable as well. So, after a visit to a college friend in Vancouver for a birthday weekend, she'd decided she loved the city. She gave her notice to Jeremy and moved out to B.C. within a month. She'd taken the job at the bar to make ends meet while looking for something more permanent. Honestly, she had just wanted to have some fun, hang out at a good place, and earn some cash while she crashed at her friend's place temporarily. It was never intended as a long-term thing, and Olivia wasn't looking to build a career serving drinks at happy hour, though it was well suited to her outgoing personality.

"Olivia, what would you say if I told you *I'm* looking for somebody to make it rain? Somebody who knows and loves cars? And somebody with some sales experience?" Kevin asked.

Olivia nearly dropped her drink tray.

"I understand you may not have an up-to-date résumé prepared, because you probably haven't been looking for a sales job recently, but I'd like to talk to you about who I'm looking for and what you're looking for. Would you be willing to meet with me?"

When Olivia showed up at his office three days later, Kevin had a photograph of a red '69 Camaro on his wall with her name on it.

Prior to beginning the interview process, Kevin said, "Olivia, if I read you right the other evening and you really dream of owning one of these someday, the owner of this company and I can give you that opportunity."

That's when Olivia's eyes lit up as if the sun lived inside her soul.

The interview process Olivia experienced was the one Kevin had learned from the Impact Sales Coach training and what he had gone through personally to join the firm as a sales manager a few years prior.

It was only when he looked closely at Olivia's résumé that Kevin was stunned to discover that not only had she worked for his old employer in Chicago, but for his old friend and sales manager, Jeremy. And while he didn't feel the need to commiserate with her over his own experiences working under the "Rock Star," Kevin marveled at the coincidence: He had quit that job for what he could only assume were the same reasons Olivia had, and now here they were, in the middle of an interview 2,800 miles and a few years away from where it had all begun.

And it was all the more poignant because he'd heard from friends back home that a few months back, QAZ was still rolling along the same as ever. Earl and a couple of the hardcore old-school sales staff were still around, but Jeremy was still churning and burning through newer, younger staff just as he had with Olivia. He was still creating the conditions that turn fresh, bright-eyed, optimistic young salespeople into burned-out, disillusioned, ex-salespeople.

Ouch.

To make a long story short, Kevin offered Olivia the job and she accepted.

Kevin followed his training as a coach with a mission to grow rainmakers.

Working together with Pentagon teams, they followed the systems and processes created during Kevin's training with the coach.

They began to implement the strategic plan that he helped create with the other managers, and it worked like a charm.

They took away market share from the competition, opened new accounts, and achieved their target, hitting the double-double.

Olivia was an enthusiastic contributor to the whole group's success by sharing her creative ideas to other salespeople to help them make inroads with difficult accounts in their own territories any time questions came up in sales meetings.

In his fourth year as a manager/coach, Kevin's group of rainmakers earned the title of World Class Sales Team when they achieved a double-double for the second year in a row. The company reached its revenue targets and opened its new facility.

They were all enjoying their successes and all reaching their own personal goals, but when Olivia pulled up at the end of her second year in her red 1969, LM1 Camaro, that was the day she earned the title Rainmaker of the Year.

"Kevin, get in. Let's take it for a spin," said Olivia. "I would never have become a great rainmaker without a great rainmaker coach. Thanks for everything."

RAINMAKER PRINCIPLES
CHAPTER 18

- When people are truly passionate about something, they will never give up on their dreams.

- A manager that is disrespectful and is only driven by greed and ego will not succeed in growing any kind of team, and certainly not a championship team.

- When a company makes a mistake by promoting or hiring the wrong person for the wrong seat on the bus, they need to move that person to the right seat, or off the bus.

- The best companies with great leadership work at growing their managers to become rainmaker coaches. These coaches are always pushing to learn more about everything from human psychology to leadership history to tomorrow's technology. They dedicate themselves to the lifelong pursuit of learning more about business and incorporating best practices from around the globe. They are always keenly listening to understand, communicate and blend the unique powers and skills that millennials, Gen Xers, and boomers bring to the table.

APPENDIX

Resources

To access the items in the list below, which were discussed in Part III of this book, visit www.Growing Rainmakers.com/resources

1. eMatrix Samples

2. eMatrix Template

3. eMatrix examples of Competencies and Criteria

4. eMatrix Criteria, Definitions and Ranking Template

5. eMatrix Performance Improvement Plan Template

6. Question Guide Template and Samples

7. Success Story Guide and Sample

8. Pentagon Team Structure Diagram

9. The Seven Magic Words for Presentations

Acknowledgements

Thank you first and foremost to my wife and partner, Kathy, for all her patience, wisdom, encouragement, endless help, understanding, forgiveness and belief in me through more than three decades of marriage together. We are blessed with our three highly intelligent, loving, talented and successful daughters that have shown me many things. Rachel, Erica and Amanda are responsible for opening my eyes to the power potential of millennials and have helped me understand how to bridge the generation gaps.

I want to recognize and thank all three of my "girlies" for their individual time and help with this project. Rachel's input consistently challenged how I looked at things, combined with her creative suggestions that helped solidify my thoughts. Her gift of writing the book's foreword was an awesome surprise. Erica's fastidious use of her language skills, spelling, and communication improved the final product beyond belief. She also provided priceless help creating some of my book marketing speeches and then gave me her invaluable coaching to help bring the story to life. Amanda's job was the toughest one of all. She whisked me around St. Louis, taking hundreds of photographs to find one that could go on the back cover. Not to mention all the photo editing to make it the best it could be. I love you all from the bottom of my heart, appreciate all of your help and support on this project, and the many things that you beautiful women have done to make my world a better place.

A special thankfulness, recognition and love goes out to my daughter-in-law Torre. She was my book writing coach and cheerleader for this endeavor. As an author herself, she gets it. I hope that someday you will read some of her work. My world is a much better place with daughter number four in my life.

There are many other characters that played behind-the-scenes parts in this tale. My heartfelt thanks go out to all those sales professionals, sales managers, various business leaders and rainmakers that I have worked with over my career. While their names have been changed in this tale, many of them played a role that inspired the creation of the characters in this book. A special tip of my hat goes out to my dear friend Dave Provinciano for his unwavering support of my program and ideas. I am so grateful for his support, friendship and dedicated staff of managers, the incredible director of sales and a variety of sales professionals that he allowed me to work with, grow into rainmakers and build into a *world-class sales team.*

About the Author

Over the past twenty years, Dave Wilens has run Impact Sales Coach with his wife Kathy as his partner. He has worked with companies from more than forty industries, coaching hundreds of sales managers and sales professionals to become rainmakers. As a professional author and speaker, he talks about sales, sales management, leadership, strategic planning and creating a coaching culture to grow rainmakers.

Dave's work as a coach and a speaker have taken him all over the United States, Canada, and Australia, while one-to-one virtual coaching has allowed him to mentor others all over the world. Entrepreneur's Organization (EO), TEC and Vistage are a few of the organizations that hire him as a guest speaker to educate business owners and leaders. As a business owner and previous TEC member himself, he doesn't believe it makes sense to jazz people up as a subject-matter expert and then leave them to figure out how to do it on their own. So, many of these leaders bring him in to work directly with their teams in the field, office, virtually or for large sales/management meetings.

On a personal note, Dave enjoys live music and theater performances, especially if one of his daughters is performing; traveling with his wife; good food paired with great wine; and golfing whenever and wherever possible.

Most of all he enjoys spending time with his family, friends, and clients (who usually become his friends).

To contact Dave for speaking, coaching, strategic planning, or bulk orders of this book (twenty-five or more), email him at CoachDave@ImpactSalesCoach. com or visit GrowingRainmakers.com

Made in the USA
San Bernardino, CA
14 April 2019